TRYING TO FIND CHINATOWN

The Selected Plays

David Henry Hwang

THEATRE COMMUNICATIONS GROUP

Trying to Find Chinatown: The Selected Plays of David Henry Hwang is published by Theatre Communications Group, Inc., 355 Lexington Ave., New York, NY 10017–6603.

The House of Sleeping Beauties is adapted from a short story by Yasunari Kawabata, 1961. The biblical quotes within Act II, Scene One, of *The Voyage* are from Ecclesiasticus 43:26, Luke 10:23, Zechariah 9:10 and Isaiah 49:23, respectivley; Act II, Scene Two's translations and nautical terms are from Samuel Eliot Morrison's *Admiral of the Ocean Sea*, 1942.

This publication is made possible in part with public funds from the New York State Council on the Arts, a State Agency.

TCG books are exclusively distributed to the book trade by Consortium Book Sales and Distribution, 1045 Westgate Dr., St. Paul, MN 55114.

LIBRARY OF CONGRESS CATALOGING-IN-PUBLICATION DATA

Hwang, David Henry, 1957–
Trying to find Chinatown : the selected plays of David Henry Hwang / by David Henry Hwang. — 1st ed.
p. cm.
ISBN 978-1-55936-172-9
1. America—Discovery and exploration—Drama. 2. United States— Race relations—Drama. 3. Asian Americans—Drama. 4. Asia—Drama. I. Title.
PS3558.W83 A6   1999
812'.54—dc21   99-044197

Book design and typography by Lisa Govan
Cover photo by Susan Johann
Cover design by Carol Devine Carson

First edition, June 2000
Third Printing, March 2021

CONTENTS

FOB

(1980)

For the warriors of my family

Production History

FOB received its premiere at the Stanford Asian American Theatre Project (Nancy Takahashi, Producer) in Palo Alto, California, on March 2, 1979. It was directed by David Henry Hwang; the assistant director was Randall Tong; the set design was by George Prince; the costume design was by Kathy Ko and the lighting design was by Roger Tang. The cast was as follows:

DALE	Loren Fong
GRACE	Hope Nakamura
STEVE	David Pating

The play was then developed at the Eugene O'Neill National Playwrights Conference (Lloyd Richards, Artistic Director) in Waterford, Connecticut, in July 1979. It was directed by Robert Alan Ackerman. The cast was as follows:

DALE	Calvin Jung
GRACE	Ginny Yang
STEVE	Ernest Abuba

FOB opened at The Joseph Papp Public Theater/New York Shakespeare Festival (Joseph Papp, Producer), in New York City on June 8, 1980. It was directed by Mako; the assistant director was David Oyama; the set design was by Akira Yoshimura and James E. Mayo; the costume design was by Susan Hum; the lighting design was by Victor En Yu Tan; the choreography was by John Lone; the music was by Lucia Hwong; and the stage manager was Ruth Kreshka. There were also two onstage stage managers, Willy Corpus and Tzi Ma, as well as an onstage musician, Lucia Hwong, in this production. The cast was as follows:

DALE	Calvin Jung
GRACE	Ginny Yang
STEVE	John Lone

Characters

DALE, a second-generation American of Chinese descent, early twenties.
GRACE, Dale's cousin, a first-generation Chinese-American, early twenties.
STEVE, Grace's friend, a Chinese newcomer, early twenties.

Place

The back room of a small Chinese restaurant in Torrance, California.

Time

1980.

ACT I, *Scene One:* late afternoon.
     Scene Two: a few minutes later.
ACT II: after dinner.

Definitions

chong you bing is a type of Chinese pancake, a Northern Chinese appetizer often made with dough and scallions, with a consistency similar to that of pita bread.
da dao and *mao* are two swords, the traditional weapons of Gwan Gung and Fa Mu Lan, respectively.
Gung Gung means "grandfather."
Mei Guo means "beautiful country" and is a Chinese term for America.

Playwright's Note

The roots of *FOB* are thoroughly American. The play began when a sketch I was writing about a limousine trip through Westwood, California, was invaded by two figures from American literature: Fa Mu Lan, the girl who takes her father's place in battle, from Maxine Hong Kingston's *The Woman Warrior*, and Gwan Gung, the god of fighters and writers, from Frank Chin's *Gee, Pop!*

These books testify to the existence of an Asian-American literary tradition. Japanese-Americans, for instance, wrote plays in American concentration camps during World War II. Earlier, with the emergence of the railroads, came regular performances of Cantonese operas featuring Gwan Gung, the adopted god of Chinese America.

Prologue

Lights up on a blackboard. Dale enters, dressed in preppie clothes. The blackboard is the type which can flip around so both sides can be used. Dale lectures like a university professor, using the board to illustrate his points.

DALE: F-O-B. Fresh Off the Boat. FOB. What words can you think of that characterize the FOB? Clumsy, ugly, greasy FOB. Loud, stupid, four-eyed FOB. Big feet. Horny. Like Lenny in *Of Mice and Men*. Very good. A literary reference. High-water pants. Floods, to be exact. Someone you wouldn't want your sister to marry. If you are a sister, someone you wouldn't want to marry. That assumes we're talking about boy FOBs, of course. But girl FOBs aren't really as . . . FOBish. Boy FOBs are the worst, the . . . pits. They are the sworn enemies of all ABC—oh, that's "American-Born Chinese"—of all ABC girls. Before an ABC girl will be seen on a Friday night with a boy FOB in Westwood, she would rather burn off her face.

(He flips around the board. On the other side is written: "1. Where to Find FOBs. 2. How to Spot a FOB.")

FOBs can be found in great numbers almost anyplace you happen to be, but there are some locations where they cluster in particularly large swarms. Community colleges, Chinese club discos, Asian sororities, Asian fraternities, Oriental churches, shopping malls and, of course, Bee Gee concerts. How can you spot a FOB? Look out! If you can't answer that, you might be one.

(He flips back the board, reviews) F-O-B. Fresh Off the Boat. FOB. Clumsy, ugly, greasy FOB. Loud, stupid, four-eyed FOB. Big feet. Horny. Like Lenny in *Of Mice and Men*. Floods. Like Lenny in *Of Mice and Men*. F-O-B. Fresh Off the Boat. FOB.

(Lights fade to black. We hear American pop music, preferably funk, rhythm and blues, or disco.)

ACT I

Scene One

*Late afternoon. The back room of a small Chinese restau-
rant in Torrance, California. Single table, with a tablecloth;
various chairs, supplies. One door leads outside, a back exit;
another leads to the kitchen. Lights up on Grace, at the table.
The music is coming from a small radio. On the table is a
small, partially wrapped box and a huge blob of discarded
Scotch tape. As Grace tries to wrap the box, we see what has
been happening: the tape she's using is stuck in the dispenser;
so, in order to pull it out, she must tug so hard that an unus-
able quantity of tape is dispensed. Steve enters from the back
door, unnoticed by Grace. He stands, waiting to catch her
eye, tries to speak, but his voice is drowned out by the music.
He is dressed in a stylish summer outfit.*

GRACE: Aaaai-ya!
STEVE: Hey!

> *(No response; he turns off the music.)*

GRACE: Huh? Look. Out of tape.
STEVE *(In Chinese)*: Yeah.
GRACE: One whole roll. You know how much of it got on
here? Look. That much. That's all.
STEVE *(In Chinese)*: Yeah. Do you serve *chong you bing*
today?
GRACE *(Picking up box)*: Could've skipped the wrapping
paper, just covered it with tape.
STEVE *(In Chinese)*: Excuse me!

GRACE: Yeah? *(Pause)* You wouldn't have any on you, would ya?

STEVE *(Speaking English from now onward)*: Sorry? No. I don't have *bing*. I want to buy *bing*.

GRACE: Not *bing*! Tape. Have you got any tape?

STEVE: Tape? Of course I don't have tape.

GRACE: Just checking.

STEVE: Do you have any *bing*?

(Pause.)

GRACE: Look, we're closed 'til five . . .

STEVE: Idiot girl.

GRACE: Why don't you take a menu?

STEVE: I want you to tell me!

(Pause.)

GRACE *(Ignoring Steve)*: Working in a Chinese restaurant, you learn to deal with obnoxious customers.

STEVE: Hey! You!

GRACE: If the customer's Chinese, you insult them by giving forks.

STEVE: I said I want you to tell me!

GRACE: If the customer's Anglo, you starve them by not giving forks.

STEVE: You serve *bing* or not?

GRACE: But it's always easy just to dump whatever happens to be in your hands at the moment.

(She sticks the tape blob on Steve's face.)

STEVE: I suggest you answer my question at once!

GRACE: And I suggest you grab a menu and start doing things for yourself. Look, I'll get you one, even. How's that?

STEVE: I want it from your mouth!

GRACE: Sorry. We don't keep 'em there.

STEVE: If I say they are there, they are there. *(He grabs her box)*

GRACE: What—what're you doing? Give that back to me!

(They parry around the table.)

STEVE: Aaaah! Now it's different, isn't it? Now you're listening to me.

GRACE: 'Scuse me, but you really are an asshole, you know that? Who do you think you are?

STEVE: What are you asking me? Who I am?

GRACE: Yes. You take it easy with that, hear?

STEVE: You ask who *I* am?

GRACE: One more second and I'm gonna call the cops.

STEVE: Very well, I will tell you.

(She picks up the phone. He slams it down.)

I said, I'll tell you.

GRACE: If this is how you go around meeting people, I think it's pretty screwed.

STEVE: Silence! I am Gwan Gung! God of warriors, writers and prostitutes!

(Pause.)

GRACE: Bullshit!

STEVE: What?

GRACE: Bullshit! Bull-shit! You are not Gwan Gung. And gimme back my box.

STEVE: I am Gwan Gung. Perhaps we should see what you have in here.

GRACE: Don't open that! *(Beat)* You don't look like Gwan Gung. Gwan Gung is a warrior.

STEVE: I am a warrior!

GRACE: Yeah? Why are you so scrawny, then? You wouldn't last a day in battle.

STEVE: My credit! Many a larger man has been humiliated by the strength in one of my size.

GRACE: Tell me, then. Tell me, if you are Gwan Gung. Tell me of your battles. Of one battle. Of Gwan Gung's favorite battle.

STEVE: Very well. Here is a living memory: one day, Gwan Gung woke up and saw the ring of fire around the sun and decided, "This is a good day to slay villagers." So he got up, washed himself and looked over a map of the Three Kingdoms to decide where first to go. For those were days of rebellion and falling empires, so opportunity to slay was abundant. But planned slaughter required an order and restraint which soon became tedious. So Gwan Gung decided a change was in order. He called for his tailor, who he asked to make a beautiful blindfold of layered silk, fine enough to be weightless, yet thick enough to blind the wearer completely. The tailor complied, and soon produced a perfect piece of red silk, exactly suited to Gwan Gung's demands. In gratitude, Gwan Gung stayed the tailor's execution sentence. He then put on his blindfold, pulled out his sword, and began passing over the land, swiping at whatever got in his path. You see, Gwan Gung figured there was so much revenge and so much evil in those days that he could slay at random and still stand a good chance of fulfilling justice. This worked very well until his sword, in its blind fury, hit upon an old and irritable atom bomb.

(Grace catches Steve, takes back the box.)

GRACE: Ha! Some Gwan Gung you are! Some warrior you are! You can't even protect a tiny box from the grasp of a woman! How could you have shielded your big head in battle?

STEVE: Shield! Shield! I still go to battle!

GRACE: Only your head goes to battle, 'cause only your head is Gwan Gung.

(Pause.)

STEVE: You made me think of you as a quiet listener. A good trick. What is your name?

GRACE: You can call me "The Woman Who Has Defeated Gwan Gung," if that's really who you are.

STEVE: Very well. But that name will change before long.

GRACE: That story you told—that wasn't a Gwan Gung story.

STEVE: What—you think you know all of my adventures through stories? All the books in the world couldn't record the life of one man, let alone a god. Now—do you serve *bing*?

GRACE: I won the battle; you go look yourself. There.

STEVE: You working here?

GRACE: Part-time. It's my father's place. I'm also in school.

STEVE: School? University?

GRACE: Yeah. UCLA.

STEVE: Excellent. I have also come to America for school.

GRACE: Well, what use would Gwan Gung have for school?

STEVE: Wisdom. Wisdom makes a warrior stronger.

GRACE: Pretty good. If you are Gwan Gung, you're not the dumb jock I was expecting. Got a lot to learn about school, though.

STEVE: Expecting? You were expecting me?

GRACE *(Quickly)*: No, no. I meant, what I expected from the stories.

STEVE: Tell me, how do people think of Gwan Gung in America? Do they shout my name while rushing into battle, or is it too sacred to be used in such ostentatious display?

GRACE: Uh—no.

STEVE: No—what? I didn't ask a "no" question.

GRACE: What I mean is, neither. They don't do either of those.

STEVE: Not good. The name of Gwan Gung has been restricted for the use of leaders only?

GRACE: Uh—no. I think you better sit down.

STEVE: This is very scandalous. How are the people to take my strength? Gwan Gung might as well not exist, for all they know.

GRACE: You got it.

STEVE: I got what? You seem to be having trouble making your answers fit my questions.

GRACE: No, I think you're having trouble making your questions fit my answers.

STEVE: What is this nonsense? Speak clearly, or don't speak at all.

GRACE: Speak clearly?

STEVE: Yes. Like a warrior.

GRACE: Well, you see, Gwan Gung, god of warriors, writers and prostitutes, no one gives a wipe about you 'round here. You're dead.

(Pause.)

STEVE: You . . . you make me laugh.

GRACE: You died way back . . . hell, no one even noticed when you died—that's how bad off your PR was. You died and no one even missed a burp.

STEVE: You lie! The name of Gwan Gung must be feared around the world—you jeopardize your health with such remarks. *(Pause)* You—you have heard of me, I see. How can you say—?

GRACE: Oh, I just study it a lot—Chinese-American history, I mean.

STEVE: Ah. In the schools, in the universities, where new leaders are born, they study my ways.

GRACE: Well, fifteen of us do.

STEVE: Fifteen. Fifteen of the brightest, of the most promising?

GRACE: One wants to be a dental technician.

STEVE: A man studies Gwan Gung in order to clean teeth?

GRACE: There's also a middle-aged woman that's kinda bored with her kids.

STEVE: I refuse—I don't believe you—your stories. You're just angry at me for treating you like a servant. You're trying to sap my faith. The people—the people outside—they know me—they know the deeds of Gwan Gung.

GRACE: Check it out yourself.

STEVE: Very well. You will learn—learn not to test the spirit of Gwan Gung.

(Steve exits. Grace picks up the box. She studies it.)

GRACE: Fa Mu Lan sits and waits. She learns to be still while the emperors, the dynasties, the foreign lands flow past, unaware of her slender form, thinking it a tree in the woods, a statue to a goddess long abandoned by her people. But Fa Mu Lan, the Woman Warrior, is not ashamed. She knows that one who can exist without movement while the ages pass is the one to whom no victory can be denied. It is training, to wait. And Fa Mu Lan, the Woman Warrior, must train, for she is no goddess, but girl—girl who takes her father's place in battle. No goddess, but woman—warrior-woman *(She breaks through the box's wrapping, reaches in and pulls out another box, beautifully wrapped and ribboned)* —and ghost. *(She puts the new box on a shelf, goes to the phone, dials)* Hi, Dale? Hi, this is Grace . . . Pretty good. How 'bout you? . . . Good, good. Hey, listen, I'm sorry to ask you at the last minute and everything, but are you doing anything tonight? . . . Are you sure? . . . Oh, good. Would you like to go out with me and some of my friends? . . . Just out to dinner, then maybe we were thinking of going to a movie or something . . . Oh, good . . . Are you sure? . . . Yeah, okay. Um, we're all going to meet at the restaurant . . . No, *our* restaurant . . . right—as soon as possible. Okay, good . . . I'm really glad that you're coming. Sorry it's such short notice. Okay. Bye, now . . . Huh? Frank? Oh, okay. *(Pause)* Hi, Frank . . . Pretty good . . . Yeah? . . . No, I don't think so . . . Yeah . . . No, I'm sorry, I'd still rather not . . . I don't want to, okay? Do I have to be any clearer than that? . . . You are not! . . . You don't even know when they come—you'd have to lie on those tracks for hours . . . Forget it, okay? . . . Look, I'll get you a schedule so you can time it properly . . . It's not a favor, damn it. Now good-bye! *(She hangs up) Jesus!*

(Steve enters.)

STEVE: Buncha weak boys, what do they know? One man—Chinaman—wearing a leisure suit—green! I ask him, "You know Gwan Gung?" He says, "Hong Kong?" I say, "No, no. Gwan Gung." He says, "Yeah. They got sixty thousand people living on four acres. Went there last year." I say, "No, no. Gwan Gung." He says, "Ooooh! Gwan Gung?" I say, "Yes, yes, Gwan Gung." He says, "I never been there before."

GRACE: See? Even if you didn't die—who cares?

STEVE: Another kid—blue jeans and a T-shirt—I ask him, does he know Gwan Gung? He says, he doesn't need it, he knows Jesus Christ. What city is this now?

GRACE: Los Angeles.

STEVE: This isn't the only place where a new Chinaman can land, is it?

GRACE: I guess a lot go to San Francisco.

STEVE: Good. This place got a bunch of weirdos around here.

GRACE: Yeah.

STEVE: They could never be followers of Gwan Gung. All who follow me must be loyal and righteous.

GRACE: Maybe you should try some other state.

STEVE: Huh? What you say?

GRACE: Never mind. You'll get used to it—like the rest of us.

(Pause. Steve begins laughing.)

STEVE: You are a very clever woman.

GRACE: Just average.

STEVE: No. You do a good job to make it seem like Gwan Gung has no followers here. At the university, what do you study?

GRACE: Journalism.

STEVE: Journalism—you are a writer, then?

GRACE: Of a sort.

STEVE: Very good. You are close to Gwan Gung's heart.

GRACE: As close as I'm gonna get.

STEVE: I would like to go out tonight with you.

GRACE: I knew it. Look, I've heard a lot of lines before, and yours is very creative, but . . .

STEVE: I will take you out.

GRACE: You will, huh?

STEVE: I do so because I find you worthy to be favored.

GRACE: You're starting to sound like any other guy now.

STEVE: I'm sorry?

GRACE: Look—if you're going to have any kinds of relationships with women in this country, you better learn to give us some respect.

STEVE: Respect? I give respect.

GRACE: The pushy, aggressive type is out, understand?

STEVE: Taking you out is among my highest tokens of respect.

GRACE: Oh, c'mon—they dont even say that in Hong Kong.

STEVE: You are being asked out by Gwan Gung!

GRACE: I told you, you're too wimpy to be Gwan Gung. And even if you were, you'd have to wait your turn in line.

STEVE: What?

GRACE: I already have something for tonight. My cousin and I are having dinner.

STEVE: You would turn down Gwan Gung for your cousin?

GRACE: Well, he has an X-19.

(*Pause.*)

STEVE: What has happened?

GRACE: Look—I tell you what. If you take both of us out, then it'll be okay, all right?

STEVE: I don't want to go out with your cousin!

GRACE: Well, sorry. It's part of the deal.

STEVE: Deal? What deals? Why am I made part of these deals?

GRACE: 'Cause you're in the U.S. in 1980, just like the rest of us. Now quit complaining. Will you take it or not?

(Pause.)

STEVE: Gwan Gung . . . bows to no one's terms but his own.
GRACE: Fine. Why don't you go down the street to Imperial
    Dragon Restaurant and see if they have *bing*?
STEVE: Do you have *bing*?
GRACE: See for yourself.

(She hands him a menu. He exits. Grace picks up the box.)

Fa Mu Lan stood in the center of the village and
turned 'round and 'round as the bits of fingers, the tips
of tongues, the arms, the legs, the peeled skulls, the
torn maidenheads, all whirled by. She pulled the loose
gown closer to her body, stepped over the torsos, in
search of the one of her family who might still be
alive. Reaching the house that was once her home,
crushing bones in her haste, only to find the doorway
covered with the stretched and dried skin of that
which was once her father. Climbing through an open
window, noticing the shiny, black, thousand-day-old
egg still floating in the shiny black sauce. Finding her
sister tied spread-eagle on the mat, finding her mother
in the basket in pieces, finding her brother nowhere.
The Woman Warrior went to the mirror, which had
stayed unbroken, and let her gown come loose and drop
to the ground. She turned and studied the ideographs
that had long ago been carved into the flesh of her
young back . . . Carved by her mother, who lay carved
in the basket.

(Dale enters, approaches Grace.)

She ran her fingers over the skin and felt the ridges
where there had been pain.

(Dale is behind Grace.)

But now they were firm and hard.

(*Dale touches Grace, who reacts by swinging around and knocking him to the ground. Only after he is down does she see his face.*)

Dale! Shit! I'm sorry. I didn't . . . !

DALE (*Groggy*): Am I late?

GRACE: I didn't know it was you, Dale.

DALE: Yeah. Well, I didn't announce myself.

GRACE: You shouldn't just come in here like that.

DALE: You're right. Never again.

GRACE: I mean, you should've yelled from the dining room.

DALE: Dangerous neighborhood, huh?

GRACE: I'm so sorry. Really.

DALE: Yeah. Uh—where're your other friends? They on the floor around here too?

GRACE: No. Uh—this is really bad, Dale. I'm really sorry.

DALE: What?—You can't make it after all?

GRACE: No, I can make it. It's just that . . .

DALE: They can't make it? Okay, so it'll just be us. That's cool.

GRACE: Well, not quite us.

DALE: Oh.

GRACE: See, what happened is—you know my friend Judy?

DALE: Uh—no.

GRACE: Well, she was gonna come with us—with me and this guy I know—his name is . . . Steve.

DALE: Oh, he's with you, right?

GRACE: Well, sort of. So since she was gonna come, I thought you should come too.

DALE: To even out the couples?

GRACE: But now my friend Judy, she decided she had too much work to do, so . . . oh, it's all messed up.

DALE: Well, that's okay. I can go home—or I can go out with you, if this guy Steve doesn't mind. Where is he, anyway?

GRACE: I guess he's late. You know, he just came to this country.

DALE: Oh yeah? How'd you meet him?

GRACE: At a Chinese dance at UCLA.

DALE: Hmmmm. Some of those FOBs get moving pretty fast.

(Grace glares.)

Oh. Is he . . . nice?

GRACE: He's okay. I don't know him that well. You know, I'm really sorry.

DALE: Hey, I said it was okay. Jesus, it's not like you hurt me or anything.

GRACE: For that, too.

DALE: Look— *(He hits himself)* No pain!

GRACE: What I meant was, I'm sorry tonight's got so messed up.

DALE: Oh, it's okay. I wasn't doing anything anyway.

GRACE: I know, but still . . .

(Silence.)

DALE: Hey, that Frank is a joke, huh?

GRACE: Yeah. He's kind of a pain.

DALE: Yeah. What an asshole to call my friend.

GRACE: Did you hear him on the phone?

DALE: Yeah, all that railroad stuff?

GRACE: It was real dumb.

DALE: Dumb? He's dumb. He's doing it right now.

GRACE: Huh? Are you serious?

DALE: Yeah. I'm tempted to tie him down so, for once in his life, he won't screw something up.

GRACE: You're kidding!

DALE: Huh? Yeah, sure I'm kidding. Who would I go bowling with?

GRACE: No, I mean about him actually going out there—is that true?

DALE: Yeah—he's lying there. You know, right on Torrance Boulevard?

GRACE: No!

DALE: Yeah!

GRACE: But what if a train really comes?

DALE: I dunno. I guess he'll get up.

GRACE: I don't believe it!

DALE: Unless he's fallen asleep by that time or something.

GRACE: He's crazy.

DALE: Which is a real possibility for Frank, he's such a bore anyway.

GRACE: He's weird.

DALE: No, he just thinks he's in love with you.

GRACE: Is he?

DALE: I dunno. We'll see when the train comes.

GRACE: Do you think we should do something?

DALE: What?—You're not gonna fall for the twerp, are you?

GRACE: Well, no, but . . .

DALE: He's stupid—and ugly, to boot.

GRACE: . . . but staying on the tracks is kinda dangerous.

DALE: Let him. Teach him a lesson.

GRACE: You serious?

DALE *(Moving closer to Grace)*: Not to fool with my cousin.

(He strokes her hair. They freeze in place, except for his arm, which continues to stroke her hair. Steve enters, oblivious of Dale and Grace, who do not respond to him. He speaks to the audience as if it were a panel of judges:)

STEVE: No! Please! Listen to me! This is fifth time I come here. I tell you both my parents, I tell you their parents, I tell you their parents' parents and who was adopted great-granduncle. I tell you how many beggars in hometown and name of their blind dogs. I tell you number of steps from my front door to temple, to well, to governor house, to fields, to whorehouse, to fifth cousin inn, to eighth neighbor toilet—you ask only: what for am I in whorehouse? I tell north, south, northeast, southwest, west, east, north-northeast, south-southwest, east-eastsouth—why will you not let me enter in America? I come here five times—I raise

21

lifetime fortune five times. Five times, I first come here, you say to me I am illegal, you return me on boat to fathers and uncles with no gold, no treasure, no fortune, no rice. I only want to come to America—come to "Mountain of Gold." And I hate Mountain and I hate America and I hate you! *(Pause)* But this year you call 1914—very bad for China.

(Pause; lights shift. Grace and Dale become mobile and aware of Steve's presence.)

GRACE: Oh! Steve, this is Dale, my cousin. Dale, Steve.

DALE: Hey, nice to meet . . .

STEVE *(Now speaking English with a Chinese accent)*: Hello. Thank you. I am fine.

(Pause.)

DALE: Uh, yeah. Me too. So, you just got here, huh? What'cha think?

(Steve smiles and nods; Dale smiles and nods. Steve laughs; Dale laughs. Steve hits Dale on the shoulder. They laugh some more. They stop laughing.)

Oh. Uh—good. *(Pause)* Well, it looks like it's just gonna be the three of us, right? *(To Grace)* Where you wanna go?

GRACE: I think Steve's already taken care of that. Right, Steve?

STEVE: Excuse?

GRACE: You made reservations at a restaurant?

STEVE: Oh, reservations. Yes, yes.

DALE: Oh, okay. That limits the possibilities. Guess we're going to Chinatown or something, right?

GRACE *(To Steve)*: Where is the restaurant?

STEVE: Oh. The restaurant is a French restaurant. Los Angeles downtown.

DALE: Oh, we're going to a Western place? *(To Grace)* Are you sure he made reservations?

GRACE: We'll see.

DALE: Well, I'll get my car.

GRACE: Okay.

STEVE: No!

DALE: Huh?

STEVE: Please—allow me to provide car.

DALE: Oh. You wanna drive.

STEVE: Yes. I have car.

DALE: Look—why don't you let me drive? You've got enough to do without worrying about—you know— how to get around L.A., read the stop signs, all that.

STEVE: Please—allow me to provide car. No problem.

DALE: Well, let's ask Grace, okay? *(To Grace)* Grace, who do you think should drive?

GRACE: I don't really care. Why don't you two figure it out? But let's hurry, okay? We open pretty soon.

DALE *(To Steve)*: Look—you had to pick the restaurant we're going to, so the least I can do is drive.

STEVE: Uh, your car—how many people sit in it?

DALE: Well, it depends. Right now, none.

GRACE *(To Dale)*: He's got a point. You car only seats two.

DALE: He can sit in the back. There's space there. I've fit luggage in it before.

GRACE *(To Steve)*: You want to sit in the back?

STEVE: I sit—where?

DALE: Really big suitcases.

GRACE: Back of his car.

STEVE: X-19? Aaaai-ya!

DALE: X-19?

STEVE: No deal!

DALE: How'd he know that? How'd he know what I drive?

STEVE: Please. Use my car. Is . . . big.

DALE: Yeah? Well, how much room you got? *(Pause; slower)* How-big-your-car-is?

STEVE: Huh?

DALE: Your car—how is big?

GRACE: How big is your car?

STEVE: Oh! You go see.

DALE: 'Cause if it's, like, a Pinto or something, it's not that much of a difference.

STEVE: Big and black. Outside.

GRACE: Let's hurry.

DALE: Sure, sure. *(Exits)*

GRACE: What are you up to, anyway?

STEVE *(Dropping accent)*: Gwan Gung will not go into battle without equipment worthy of his position.

GRACE: Position? You came back, didn't you? What does that make you?

DALE *(Entering)*: Okay. There's only one black car out there—

STEVE *(Resumes speaking English with an accent)*: Black car is mine.

DALE: —and that's a Fleetwood limo. Now, you're not gonna tell me that's his.

STEVE: Cadillac. Cadillac is mine.

DALE: Limousine . . . Limousine is yours?

STEVE: Yes, yes. Limousine.

(Pause.)

DALE *(To Grace)*: You wanna ride in that black thing? People will think we're dead.

GRACE: It does have more room.

DALE: Well, it has to. It's built for passengers who can't bend.

GRACE: And the driver *is* expensive.

DALE: He could go home—save all that money.

GRACE: Well, I don't know. You decide.

DALE *(To Steve)*: Look, we take my car, savvy?

STEVE: Please—drive my car.

DALE: I'm not trying to be unreasonable or anything.

STEVE: My car—just outside.

DALE: I know where it is, I just don't know why it is.

GRACE: Steve's father manufactures souvenirs in Hong Kong.

DALE *(To Steve)*: Oh, and that's how you manage that out there, huh?—from thousands of aluminum Buddhas and striptease pens.

GRACE: Well, he can't drive and he has the money—
DALE *(To Grace)*: I mean, wouldn't you just feel filthy?
GRACE: —so it's easier for him.
DALE: Getting out of a limo in the middle of Westwood? People staring, thinking we're from SC? Wouldn't you feel like dirt?
GRACE: It doesn't matter to either way to me.

(Pause.)

DALE: Where's your social conscience?
GRACE: Look—I have an idea. Why don't we just stay here.
STEVE: We stay here to eat?
GRACE: No one from the restaurant will bother us, and we can bring stuff in from the kitchen.
STEVE: I ask you to go out.
DALE: Look, Grace, I can't put ya out like that.
GRACE *(To Dale)*: It's no problem, really. It should be fun.
   (To Steve) Since there are three of us—
DALE: Fun?
GRACE *(To Steve)*: —it is easier to eat here.
DALE: How can it be fun? It's cheaper.
STEVE: Does not seem right.
GRACE: I mean, unless our restaurant isn't nice enough.
DALE: No, no—that's not it.
STEVE *(Watching Dale)*: No—this place, very nice.
GRACE: Are you sure?
DALE: Yeah. Sure.
STEVE *(Imitating Dale)*: Yeah. Sure.
DALE: Do you have . . . uh—those burrito things?
GRACE: *Moo-shoo?*
DALE: Yeah, that.
GRACE: Yeah.
DALE: And black mushrooms.
GRACE: Sure.
DALE: And sea cucumber?
STEVE: Do you have *bing*?

(Pause.)

GRACE: Look, Dad and Russ and some of the others are gonna be setting up pretty soon, so let's get our place ready, okay?

DALE: Okay. Need any help?

GRACE: Well, yeah. That's what I just said.

DALE: Oh, right. I thought maybe you were just being polite.

GRACE: Yeah. Meet me in the kitchen.

DALE: Are you sure your dad won't mind?

GRACE: What?

DALE: Cooking for us.

GRACE: Oh, it's okay. He'll cook for anybody.

(Grace exits. Silence.)

DALE: So, how do you like America?

STEVE: Very nice.

DALE: "Very nice." Good, colorful, Hong Kong English. English—how much of it you got down, anyway?

STEVE: Please repeat?

DALE: English—you speak how much?

STEVE: Oh—very little.

DALE: Honest. *(Pause)* You feel like you're an American? Don't tell me. Lemme guess. Your father. *(He switches into a mock Hong Kong accent)* Your fad-dah tink he sending you here so you get yo' M.B.A., den go back and covuh da world wit' trinkets and beads. Diversify. Franchise. Sell—ah—Hong Kong X-ray glasses at tourist shop at Buckingham Palace. You know—ah— "See da Queen"? *(Switches back to American accent)* He's hoping your American education's gonna create an empire of defective goods and breakable merchandise. Like those little cameras with the slides inside? I bought one at Disneyland once and it ended up having pictures of Hong Kong in it. You know how shitty it is to expect the Magic Kingdom and wind up with the skyline of Kowloon? Part of your dad's plan, I'm sure. But you're gonna double-cross him. Coming to

America, you're gonna jump the boat. You're gonna decide you like us. Yeah—you're gonna like having fifteen theatres in three blocks, you're gonna like West Hollywood and Newport Beach. You're gonna decide to become an American. Yeah, don't deny it—it happens to the best of us. You can't hold out—you're no different. You won't even know it's coming before it has you. Before you're trying real hard to be just like the rest of us—go dinner, go movie, go motel, bang-bang. And when your father writes you that do-it-yourself acupuncture sales are down, you'll throw that letter in the basket and burn it in your brain. And you'll write that you're gonna live in Monterey Park a few years before going back home—and you'll get your green card—and you'll build up a nice little stockbroker's business and have a few American kids before your dad realizes what's happened and dies, his hopes reduced to a few chattering teeth and a pack of pornographic playing cards. Yeah—great things come to the U.S. out of Hong Kong.

(Steve lights a cigarette, blows smoke, stands.)

STEVE: Such as your parents?

(Steve turns on the radio. Blackout.)

Scene Two

Lights up on Dale and Steve eating. It is a few minutes later, and food is on the table. Dale eats Chinese-style, vigorously shoveling food into his mouth. Steve picks. Grace enters carrying a jar of hot sauce. Steve sees her.

STEVE *(To Grace)*: After eating, you like to go dance?
DALE *(Face in bowl)*: No, thanks. I think we'd be conspicuous.
STEVE *(To Grace)*: Like to go dance?

GRACE: Perhaps. We'll see.

DALE *(To Steve)*: Wait a minute. Hold on. How can you just . . . ? I'm here, too, you know. Don't forget I exist just 'cause you can't understand me.

STEVE: Please repeat?

DALE: I get better communication from my fish. Look, we go see movie. Three here, see? One, two, three. Three can see movie. Only two can dance.

GRACE: True, but . . .

DALE *(To Grace)*: That would really be a screw, you know? You invite me down here, you don't have anyone for me to go out with, but you decide to go dancing.

GRACE: Dale, I understand.

DALE: Understand? That would really be a screw. *(To Steve)* Look, if you wanna dance, go find yourself some nice FOB partner.

STEVE: "FOB"? Has what meaning?

GRACE: Dale . . .

DALE: F-O-B. Fresh Off the Boat. FOB.

GRACE: Dale, I agree.

DALE: See, we both agree. *(To Grace)* He's a pretty prime example, isn't he? All those foreign students—

GRACE: I mean, I agree about going dancing.

DALE: —go swimming in their underwear and everything—what?

GRACE *(To Steve)*: Please understand. This is not the right time for dancing.

STEVE: Okay.

DALE: "Okay." It's okay when *she* says it's okay.

STEVE *(To Dale)*: "Fresh Off Boat" has what meaning?

(Pause.)

DALE *(To Grace)*: Did you ever hear about Dad his first year in the U.S.?

GRACE: Dale, he wants to know . . .

DALE: Well, Gung Gung was pretty rich back then, so Dad must've been a pretty disgusting . . . one, too. You know, his first year here, he spent, like thirteen thousand dollars. And that was back 'round 1950.

GRACE: Well, Mom never got anything.

STEVE: FOB means what?

DALE: That's probably 'cause women didn't get anything back then. Anyway, he bought himself a new car—all kinds of stuff, I guess. But then Gung Gung went bankrupt, so Dad had to work.

GRACE: And Mom starved.

DALE: Couldn't hold down a job. Wasn't used to taking orders from anyone.

GRACE: Mom was used to taking orders from everyone.

STEVE: Please explain this meaning.

DALE: Got fired from job after job. Something like fifteen in a year. He'd just walk in the front door and out the back, practically.

GRACE: Well, at least he had a choice of doors. At least he was educated.

STEVE *(To Dale)*: Excuse!

DALE: Huh?

GRACE: He was educated. Here. In America. When Mom came over, she couldn't just quit 'cause she was mad at her employer. It was work or starve.

DALE: Well, Dad had some pretty lousy jobs, too.

STEVE *(To Dale)*: Explain, please!

GRACE: Do you know what it's like to work eighty hours a week just to feed yourself?

DALE: Do you?

STEVE: Dale!

DALE *(To Steve)*: It means you. You know how, if you go to a fish store or something, they have the stuff that just came in that day? Well, so have you.

STEVE: I do not understand.

DALE: Forget it. That's part of what makes you one.

(Pause.)

STEVE *(Picking up hot sauce, to Dale)*: Hot. You want some?

(Pause.)

DALE: Well, yeah. Okay. Sure.

(Steve puts hot sauce on Dale's food.)

Hey, isn't that kinda a lot?

GRACE: See, Steve's family comes from Shanghai.

DALE: Hmmmm. Well, I'll try it. *(He takes a gulp, then puts down his food)*

GRACE: I think perhaps that was too much for him.

DALE: No.

GRACE: Want some water?

DALE: Yes.

(Grace exits.)

You like hot sauce? You like your food hot? All right— here. *(He dumps the contents of the jar on Steve's plate, stirs)* Fucking savage. Don't you ever worry about your intestines falling out?

(Grace enters, gives water to Dale. Steve sits, shocked.)

Thanks. FOBs can eat anything, huh? They're specially trained. Helps maintain the characteristic greasy look.

(Steve, cautiously, beings to eat his food.)

What—? Look, Grace, he's eating that! He's amazing! A freak! What a cannibal!

GRACE *(Taking Dale's plate)*: Want me to throw yours out?

DALE *(Snatching it back)*: Huh? No. No, I can eat it.

(Dale and Steve stare at each other across the table. In unison, they pick up as large a glob of food as possible, stuff it into their mouths. They cough and choke. They rest, repeat the face-off a second time. They continue in silent pain. Grace, who has been watching this, speaks to the audience:)

GRACE: Yeah. It's tough trying to live in Chinatown. But it's tough trying to live in Torrance, too. It's true. I don't like being alone. You know, when Mom could finally bring me to the U.S., I was already ten. But I never studied my English very hard in Taiwan, so I got moved back to the second grade. There were a few Chinese girls in the fourth grade, but they were American-born, so they wouldn't even talk to me. They'd just stay with themselves and compare how much clothes they all had, and make fun of the way we all talked. I figured I had a better chance of getting in with the white kids than with them, so in junior high, I started bleaching my hair and hanging out at the beach—you know, Chinese hair looks pretty lousy when you bleach it. After a while, I knew what beach was gonna be good on any given day, and I could tell who was coming just by his van. But the American-born Chinese, it didn't matter to them. They just giggled and went to their own dances. Until my senior year in high school—that's how long it took for me to get over this whole thing. One night I took Dad's car and drove on Hollywood Boulevard, all the way from downtown to Beverly Hills, then back on Sunset. I was looking and listening—all the time with the window down, just so I'd feel like I was part of the city. And that Friday, it was—I guess—I said, "I'm lonely. And I don't like it. I don't like being alone." And that was all. As soon as I said it, I felt all of the breeze—it was really cool on my face—and I heard all of the radio—and the music sounded really good, you know? So I drove home.

(Pause. Dale bursts out coughing.)

Oh, I'm sorry. Want some more water, Dale?
DALE: It's okay. I'll get it myself. *(He exits)*
STEVE *(Looks at Grace)*: Good, huh?

(Steve and Grace stare at each other as lights fade to black.)

ACT II

In blackout.

DALE: I am much better now.

(Single spot on Dale.)

I go out now. Lots. I can, anyway. Sometimes I don't ask anyone, so I don't go out. But I could. *(Pause)* I am much better now. I have friends now. Lots. They drive Porsche Carreras. Well, one does. He has a house up in the Hollywood Hills where I can stand and look down on the lights of L.A. I guess I haven't really been there yet. But I could easily go. I'd just have to ask. *(Pause)* My parents—they don't know nothing about the world, about watching Benson at the Roxy, about ordering hors d'oeuvres at Scandia's, downshifting onto the Ventura Freeway at midnight. They're yellow ghosts and they've tried to cage me up with Chineseness when all the time we were in America. *(Pause)* So, I've had to work real hard—real hard—to be myself. To not be a Chinese, a yellow, a slant, a gook. To be just a human being, like everyone else. *(Pause)* I've paid my dues. And that's why I'm much better now. I'm making it, you know? I'm making it in America.

(A napkin is thrown in front of Dale's face from right. As it passes, the lights go up. The napkin falls on the dinner table from the last scene. Dale is in the back room. Dinner is over. Steve has thrown the napkin from where he is sitting in his chair. Dale is standing upstage of the table and had been talking to Steve.)

So, look, will you just not be so . . . Couldn't you just be a
little more . . . ? I mean, we don't have to do all this . . .
You know what's gonna happen to us tomorrow morning? *(He burps)* What kinda diarrhea . . . ? Look, maybe
if you could just be a little more . . . *(He gropes)* normal. Here—stand up.

(Steve does.)

Don't smile like that. Okay. You ever see *Saturday
Night Fever?*
STEVE: Oh. *Saturday* . . .
DALE: Yeah.
STEVE. Oh. *Saturday Night Fever.* Disco.
DALE: That's it. Okay. You know . . .
STEVE: John Travolta.
DALE: Right. John Travolta. Now, maybe if you could just
be a little more like him.
STEVE: Uh—Bee Gees?
DALE: Yeah, right. Bee Gees. But what I mean is . . .
STEVE: You like Bee Gees?
DALE: I dunno. They're okay. Just stand a little more like
him, you know, his walk? *(He tries to demonstrate)*
STEVE: I believe Bee Gees very good.
DALE: Yeah. Listen.
STEVE: You see movie name of . . .
DALE: Will you listen for a sec?
STEVE: . . . *Grease?*
DALE: Hold on!
STEVE: Also Bee Gees.
DALE: I'm trying to help you!
STEVE: Also John Travolta?
DALE: I'm trying to get you normal!
STEVE: And—Oliver John-Newton.
DALE: WILL YOU SHUT UP? I'M TRYING TO HELP
YOU! I'M TRYING . . .
STEVE: Very good!
DALE: . . . TO MAKE YOU LIKE JOHN TRAVOLTA!

(Dale grabs Steve by the arm. Steve coldly knocks Dale's hands away. Dale picks up the last of the dirty dishes on the table and backs into the kitchen. Grace enters from the kitchen with the wrapped box from Act I. She sits in a chair and goes over the wrapping, her back to Steve. He gets up and begins to go for the box, almost reaching her. She turns around suddenly, though, and he drops to the floor. He pretends to be looking for something. Dale, confident he's given up, goes to the kitchen. Steve resumes his attempt, but just as he reaches the kitchen door, Dale reenters with a wet sponge.)

(To Steve) Oh, you finally willing to help? I already brought in all the dishes, you know. Here—wipe the table.

(Dale gives the sponge to Steve, then returns to the kitchen. Steve throws the sponge on the floor, sits back at the table. Grace turns around, sees the sponge on the floor, picks it up and goes to wipe the table. She brings the box with her and holds it in her hand.)

GRACE: Look—you've been wanting this for some time now. Okay. Here. I'll give it to you. *(She puts the box on the table)* A welcome to the country. You don't have to fight for it—I'll give it to you instead.

(Pause; Steve pushes the box off the table.)

Okay. Your choice. *(She wipes the table)*
DALE *(Entering from kitchen; sees Grace)*: What—you doing this?
GRACE: Don't worry, Dale.
DALE: I asked him to do it.
GRACE: I'll do it.
DALE: I asked him to do it. He's useless! *(He takes the sponge)* Look, I don't know how much English you know, but *(Using a mock Chinese accent)* look-ee!
GRACE: Dale, don't do that.

DALE *(Using sponge)*: Look—makes table all clean, see?

GRACE: You have to understand . . .

DALE: Ooooh! Nice and clean!

GRACE: . . . he's not used to this.

DALE: Look! I can see myself!

GRACE: Look, I can do this. Really.

DALE: Here—now you do.

(Dale forces Steve's hand onto the sponge.)

Good. Very good. Now, move it around.

(Dale leads Steve's hand.)

Oh, you learn so fast. Get green card, no time flat, buddy.

(Dale removes his hand; Steve stops.)

Uh-uh-uh. You must do it yourself. Come. There— now doesn't that make you feel proud?

(Dale takes his hand off again; Steve stops. Dale gives up, crosses downstage. Steve remains at the table, still.)

Jesus! I'd trade him in for a vacuum cleaner any day.

GRACE: You shouldn't humiliate him like that.

DALE: What humiliate? I asked him to wipe the table, that's all.

GRACE: See, he's different. He probably has a lot of servants at home.

DALE: Big deal. He's in America, now. He'd better learn to work.

GRACE: He's rich, you know.

DALE: So what? They all are. Rich FOBs.

GRACE: Does that include me?

DALE: Huh?

GRACE: Does that include me? Am I one of your "rich FOBs"?

DALE: What? Grace, c'mon, that's ridiculous. You're not rich. I mean, you're not poor, but you're not rich either. I mean, you're not a FOB. FOBs are different. You've been over here most of your life. You've had time to thaw out. You've thawed out really well, and, besides—you're my cousin.

(Dale strokes Grace's hair, and they freeze as before. Steve, meanwhile, has almost imperceptibly begun to clean with his sponge. He speaks to the audience as if speaking with his family:)

STEVE *(Drops accent)*: Yes. I will go to America. "Mei Guo." *(Pause. He continues wiping with the sponge)* The white ghosts came into the harbor today. They promised that they would bring us to America, and that in America we would never want for anything. One white ghost told how the streets are paved with diamonds, how the land is so rich that pieces of gold lie on the road, and the worker-devils consider them too insignificant even to bend down for. They told of a land where there are no storms, no snow, but sunshine and warmth all year-round, where a man could live out in the open and feel not even discomfort from the nature around him—a worker's paradise. A land of gold, a mountain of wealth, a land in which a man can make his fortune and grow without wrinkles into an old age. And the white ghosts are providing free passage both ways. *(Pause)* All we need to do is sign a worker's contract. *(Pause)* Yes, I am going to America.

(At this point, Grace and Dale become mobile, but still fail to hear Steve. Grace picks up the box.)

DALE: What's that?

STEVE *(His wiping becomes increasingly frenzied)*: I am going to America because of its promises. I am going to follow the white ghosts because of their promises.

DALE: Is this for me?

STEVE: Because they promised! They promised! AND LOOK! YOU PROMISED! THIS IS SHIT! IT'S NOT TRUE.

DALE (*Taking the box*): Let's see what's inside, is that okay?

(*Steve shoves Dale to the ground and takes the box.*)

STEVE: IT IS NOT! (*With accent*) THIS IS MINE!

DALE: Well, what kind of shit is that?

STEVE: She gave this to me.

DALE: What kind of . . . we're not at your place. We're not in Hong Kong, you know. Look—look all around you—you see shit on the sidewalks?

STEVE: This is mine!

DALE: You see armies of rice-bowl haircuts?

STEVE: She gave this to me!

DALE: People here have their flies zipped up—see?

STEVE: You should not look in it.

DALE: So you're not in Hong Kong. And I'm not one of your servant boys that you can knock around—that you got by trading pornographic playing cards—that you probably deal out to your friends. You're in America, understand?

STEVE: Quiet! Do you know who I am?

DALE: Yeah—you're a FOB. You're a rich FOB in the U.S. But you better watch yourself. 'Cause you can be sent back.

STEVE: Shut up! Do you know who I am?

DALE: You can be sent back, you know—just like that. 'Cause you're a guest here, understand?

STEVE (*To Grace*): Tell him who I am.

DALE: I know who he is—heir to a fortune in junk merchandise. Big deal. Like being heir to Captain Crunch.

STEVE: Tell him!

(*Silence.*)

GRACE: You know it's not like that.

STEVE: Tell him!

DALE: Huh?

GRACE: All the stuff about rice bowls and—zippers—have you ever been there, Dale?

DALE: Well, yeah. Once. When I was ten.

GRACE: Well, it's changed a lot.

DALE: Remember getting heat rashes.

GRACE: People are dressing really well now—and the whole place has become really stylish—well, certainly not everybody, but the people who are well-off enough to send their kids to American colleges—they're really kinda classy.

DALE: Yeah.

GRACE: Sort of.

DALE: You mean, like him. So what? It's easy to be classy when you're rich.

GRACE: All I'm saying is . . .

DALE: Hell, I could do that.

GRACE: Huh?

DALE: I could be classy, too, if I was rich.

GRACE: You *are* rich.

DALE: No. Just upper-middle. Maybe.

GRACE: Compared to us, you're rich.

DALE: No, not really. And especially not compared to him. Besides, when I was born we were still poor.

GRACE: Well, you're rich now.

DALE: Used to get one LifeSaver a day.

GRACE: That's all? One LifeSaver?

DALE: Well, I mean, that's not all I lived on. We got normal food, too.

GRACE: I know, but . . .

DALE: Not like we were living in cardboard boxes or anything.

GRACE: All I'm saying is that the people who are coming in now—a lot of them are different—they're already Westernized. They don't act like they're fresh off the boat.

DALE: Maybe. But they're still FOBs.

STEVE: Tell him who I am!

DALE: Anyway, real nice dinner, Grace. I really enjoyed it.

GRACE: Thank you.

STEVE: Okay! I will tell myself.

DALE: Go tell yourself—just don't bother us.

GRACE *(Standing, to Steve)*: What would you like to do now?

STEVE: Huh?

GRACE: You wanted to go out after dinner?

STEVE: Yes, yes. We go out.

DALE: I'll drive. You sent the hearse home.

STEVE: I tell driver—return car after dinner.

DALE: How could you . . . ? What time did you . . . ? When did you tell him to return? What time?

STEVE *(Looks at his watch)*: Seven-five.

DALE: No—not what time is it. What time you tell him to return?

STEVE: Seven-five. Go see.

(Dale exits through the kitchen.)

(No accent) Why wouldn't you tell him who I am?

GRACE: Can Gwan Gung die?

(Pause.)

STEVE: No warrior can defeat Gwan Gung.

GRACE: Does Gwan Gung fear ghosts?

STEVE: Gwan Gung fears no ghosts.

GRACE: Ghosts of warriors?

STEVE: No warrior ghosts.

GRACE: Ghosts that avenge?

STEVE: No avenging ghosts.

GRACE: Ghosts forced into exile?

STEVE: No exiled ghosts.

GRACE: Ghosts that wait?

(Pause.)

STEVE *(Quietly)*: May I . . . take you out tonight? Maybe not tonight, but some other time? Another time? *(He strokes her hair)* What has happened?

DALE *(Entering)*: I cannot believe it . . . *(He sees them)* What do you think you're doing? *(He grabs Steve's hand. To Steve)* What . . . I step out for one second and you just go and—hell, you FOBs are sneaky. No wonder they check you so close at Immigration.

GRACE: Dale, I can really take care of myself.

DALE: Yeah? What was his hand doing, then?

GRACE: Stroking my hair.

DALE: Well, yeah. I could see that. I mean, what was it doing stroking your hair? *(Pause)* Uh, never mind. All I'm saying is . . . *(He gropes)* Jesus! If you want to be alone, why don't you just say so, huh? If that's what you really want, just say it, okay? *(Pause)* Okay. Time's up.

GRACE: Was the car out there?

DALE: Huh? Yeah. Yeah, it was. I could not believe it. I go outside and—thank God—there's no limousine. Just as I'm about to come back, I hear this sound like the roar of death and this big black shadow scrapes up beside me. I could not believe it!

STEVE *(Speaking with accent again)*: Car return—seven-five.

DALE: And when I asked him—I asked the driver, what time he'd been told to return. And he just looks at me and says, "Now."

STEVE: We go out?

DALE: What's going on here? What is this?

STEVE: Time to go.

DALE: No! Not till you explain what's going on.

STEVE *(To Grace)*: You now want to dance?

DALE *(To Grace)*: Do you understand this? Was this coincidence?

STEVE *(To Grace)*: I am told good things of American discos.

DALE *(To Grace)*: You and him just wanna go off by yourselves?

STEVE: I hear of Dillon's.

DALE: It's okay, you know.

STEVE: In Westwood.

DALE: I don't mind.

STEVE: Three—four stories.

DALE: Really.

STEVE: Live band.

DALE: Cousin.

STEVE: We go. *(He takes Grace's hand)*

DALE: He's just out to snake you, you know.

(Dale takes Grace's other hand. From this point on, almost unnoticeably, the lights begin to dim.)

GRACE: Okay! That's enough! *(She pulls away)* That's enough! I have to make all the decisions around here, don't I? When I leave it up to you two, the only place we go is in circles.

DALE: Well . . .

STEVE: No, I am suggesting place to go.

GRACE: Look, Dale, when I asked you here, what did I say we were going to do?

DALE: Uh—dinner and a movie—or something. But it was a different "we," then.

GRACE: It doesn't matter. That's what we're going to do.

DALE: I'll drive.

STEVE: My car can take us to movie.

GRACE: I think we better not drive at all. We'll stay right here. *(She removes Steve's tie. To Steve)* Do you remember this?

DALE *(Assumes Grace is talking to him)*: What—you think I borrow clothes or something? Hell, I don't even wear ties.

(Grace takes the tie, wraps it around Dale's face like a blindfold.)

Grace, what are you . . . ?

GRACE *(To Steve)*: Do you remember this?

DALE: I already told you. I don't need a closer look or nothing.

STEVE: Yes.

GRACE *(Ties the blindfold, releases it)*: Let's sit down.

DALE: Wait.

STEVE: You want me to sit here?

DALE: Grace, is he understanding you?

GRACE: Have you ever played Group Story?

STEVE: Yes, I have played that.

DALE: There—there he goes again! Grace, I'm gonna take . . .
  (He starts to remove the blindfold)

GRACE *(Stopping him)*: Dale, listen or you won't understand.

DALE: But how come *he's* understanding?

GRACE: Because he's listening.

DALE: But . . .

GRACE: Now, let's play Group Story.

DALE: Not again. Grace, that's only good when you're stoned.

GRACE: Who wants to start? Steve, you know the rules?

STEVE: Yes—I understand.

DALE: See, we're talking normal speed—and he still understood.

GRACE: Dale, would you like to start?

(Pause.)

DALE: All right.

(By this time, the lights have dimmed, throwing shadows on the stage. Throughout the following, Grace will strike two pots together to indicate each speaker change, and the ritual will gradually take on elements of Chinese opera.)

Uh, once upon a time . . . there were . . . three bears—Grace, this is ridiculous!

GRACE: Tell a story.

DALE: . . . three bears and they each had . . . cancer of the lymph nodes. Uh—and they were very sad. So the baby bear said, "I'll go to the new Cedar Sinai Hospital, where they may have a cure for this fatal illness."

GRACE: But the new Cedar Sinai Hospital happened to be two thousand miles away—across the ocean.

STEVE *(Gradually losing his Chinese accent)*: That is very far.

DALE: How did—? So, the bear tried to swim over, but his leg got chewed off by alligators—are there alligators in the Pacific Ocean?—Oh, well. So he ended up having to go for a leg *and* a cure for malignant cancer of the lymph nodes.

GRACE: When he arrived there, he came face to face with—

STEVE: With Gwan Gung, god of warriors, writers and prostitutes.

DALE: And Gwan Gung looked at the bear and said . . .

GRACE: . . . . strongly and with spirit . . .

STEVE: "One-legged bear, what are you doing on my land? You are from America, are you not?"

DALE: And the bear said, "Yes. Yes."

GRACE: And Gwan Gung replied . . .

STEVE *(Getting up)*: By stepping forward, sword drawn, ready to wound, not kill, not end it so soon. To draw it out, play it, taunt it, make it feel like a dog.

DALE: Which is probably closely related to the bear.

GRACE: Gwan Gung said—

STEVE: "When I came to America, did you lick my wounds? When I came to America, did you cure my sickness?"

DALE: And just as Gwan Gung was about to strike—

GRACE: There arrived Fa Mu Lan, the Woman Warrior.

(She stands, faces Steve. From here on in, she no longer strikes the pots together.)

"Gwan Gung."

STEVE: "What do you want? Don't interfere! Don't forget, I have gone before you into battle many times."

DALE: But Fa Mu Lan seemed not to hear Gwan Gung's warning. She stood between him and the bear, drawing out her own sword.

GRACE: "You will learn I cannot forget. I don't forget, Gwan Gung. Spare the bear and I will present gifts."

STEVE: "Very well. He is hardly worth killing."

DALE: And the bear hopped off. Fa Mu Lan pulled a parcel from beneath her gown.

(Grace removes Dale's blindfold.)

She pulled out two items.

GRACE: "This is for you." *(She hands blindfold to Steve)*

STEVE: "What is that?"

DALE: She showed him a beautiful piece of red silk, thick enough to be opaque, yet so light he barely felt it in his hands.

GRACE: "Do you remember this?"

STEVE: "Why, yes. I used this silk for sport one day. How did you get hold of it?"

DALE: Then she presented him with a second item. It was a fabric—thick and dried and brittle.

GRACE: "Do you remember this?"

STEVE *(Turning away)*: "No, no. I've never seen this before in my life. This has nothing to do with me. What is it—a dragon skin?"

DALE: Fa Mu Lan handed it to Gwan Gung.

GRACE: "Never mind. Use it—as a tablecloth. As a favor to me."

STEVE: "It's much too hard and brittle. But, to show you my graciousness in receiving—I will use it tonight!"

DALE: That night, Gwan Gung had a large banquet, at which there was plenty, even for the slaves. But Fa Mu Lan ate nothing. She waited until midnight, till Gwan Gung and the gods were full of wine and empty of sense. Sneaking behind him, she pulled out the tablecloth, waving it above her head.

GRACE *(Ripping the tablecloth from the table)*: "Gwan Gung, you foolish boy. This thing you have used tonight as a tablecloth—it is the stretched and dried skins of my fathers. My fathers, whom you slew—for sport! And you have been eating the sins—you ate them!"

STEVE: "No. I was blindfolded. I did not know."

DALE: Fa Mu Lan waved the skin before Gwan Gung's face. It smelled suddenly of death.

GRACE: "Remember the day you played? Remember? Well, eat that day, Gwan Gung."

STEVE: "I am not responsible. No. No."

(Grace throws one end of the tablecloth to Dale, who catches it. As Grace and Dale chase Steve about the stage, waving the tablecloth like a net, they act out the roles of Steve's parents.)

DALE: Yes!

GRACE: Yes!

STEVE: No!

DALE: You must!

GRACE: Go!

STEVE: Where?

DALE: To America!

GRACE: To work!

STEVE: Why?

DALE: Because!

GRACE: We need!

STEVE: No!

DALE: Why?

GRACE: Go.

STEVE: Hard!

DALE: So?

GRACE: Need.

STEVE: Far!

DALE: So?

GRACE: Need!

STEVE: Safe!

DALE: Here?

GRACE: No!

STEVE: Why?

DALE: Them. *(Points offstage)*

GRACE: Them. *(Points offstage)*

STEVE: Won't!

DALE: Must!

GRACE: Must!

STEVE: Won't!

DALE: Go!

GRACE: Go!

STEVE: Won't!

DALE: Bye!

GRACE: Bye!

STEVE: Won't!

DALE: Fare!

GRACE: Well!

(Dale and Grace drop the tablecloth over Steve, who sinks to the floor. Grace moves offstage, while Dale goes upstage and stands with his back to the audience. Silence.)

STEVE *(Begins pounding the ground)*: Noooo!

(Steve throws off the tablecloth, standing up full. Lights up full, blindingly.)

I am GWAN GUNG!

DALE *(Turning downstage suddenly)*: What . . . ?

STEVE: I HAVE COME TO THIS LAND TO STUDY!

DALE: Grace . . .

STEVE: TO STUDY THE ARTS OF WAR, OF LITERATURE, OF RIGHTEOUSNESS!

DALE: A movie's fine.

STEVE: I FOUGHT THE WARS OF THE THREE KINGDOMS!

DALE: An ordinary movie, let's go.

STEVE: I FOUGHT WITH THE FIRST PIONEERS, THE FIRST WARRIORS THAT CHOSE TO FOLLOW THE WHITE GHOSTS TO THIS LAND!

DALE: You can pick, okay?

STEVE: I WAS THEIR HERO, THEIR LEADER, THEIR FIRE!

DALE: I'll even let *him* drive, how's that?

STEVE: AND THIS LAND IS MINE! IT HAS NO RIGHT TO TREAT ME THIS WAY!

GRACE *(Offstage)*: No. Gwan Gung, *you* have no rights.

STEVE: Who's speaking?

(Grace enters with a da dao *and* mao, *two swords.)*

GRACE: It is Fa Mu Lan. You are in a new land, Gwan Gung.

STEVE: Not new—I have been here before, many times. This time, I said I will have it easy. I will come as no Chinaman before—on a plane, with money and rank.

GRACE: And?

STEVE: And—there is no change. I am still treated like this! This land . . . has no right. I AM GWAN GUNG!

GRACE: And I am Fa Mu Lan.

DALE: I'll be Chiang Kai-shek, how's that?

STEVE *(To Dale)*: You! How can you—? I came over with your parents.

GRACE *(Turning to Steve)*: We are in America. And we have a battle to fight.

(Grace tosses the da dao *to Steve. They square off.)*

STEVE: I don't want to fight you.

GRACE: You killed my family.

STEVE: You were revenged—I ate your father's sins.

GRACE: That's not revenge!

(They strike swords.)

That was only the tease.

(Strike.)

What's the point in dying if you don't know the cause of your death?

(Series of strikes. Steve falls.)

DALE: Okay! That's it!

(Grace stands over Steve, her sword pointed at his heart. Dale snatches the sword from her hands. She does not move.)

What the hell kinda movie was that?

(Dale turns his back on the couple and heads offstage. Grace uses her now-invisible sword to thrust in and out of Steve's heart once. Dale reenters.)

That's it. Game's over. Now just sit down here. Breathe. One. Two. One. Two. Air. Good stuff. Glad they made it. Right, cousin?

(Dale strokes Grace's hair. They freeze. Steve rises slowly to his knees and delivers a monologue to the audience:)

STEVE: Ssssh! Please, miss! Please—quiet! I will not hurt you, I promise. All I want is ... food ... anything. You look full of plenty. I have not eaten almost one week now, but four days past when I found one egg and I ate every piece of it—including shell. Every piece, I ate. Please. Don't you have anything extra? *(Pause)* I want to. Now. This land does not want us any more than China. But I cannot. All work was done, then the bosses said they could not send us back. And I am running, running from Eureka, running from San Francisco, running from Los Angeles. And I been eating very little. One egg, only. *(Pause)* All America wants Chinamen go home, but no one want it bad enough to pay our way. Now, please, can't you give even little? *(Pause)* I ask you, what you hate most? What work most awful for white woman? *(Pause)* Good. I will do that thing for you—you can give me food. *(Pause)* Think—you relax, you are given those things, clean, dry, press. No scrub, no dry. It is wonderful thing I offer you. *(Pause)* Good. Give me those and please bring food, or I be done before these things.

(Grace picks up the box and steps away from Dale.)

GRACE: Here—I've brought you something. *(She hands the box to Steve)* Open it.

(Steve hesitates, then opens the box and takes out a small chong you bing.)

Eat it.

(He does, slowly at first, then ravenously.)

Good. Eat it all down. It's just food. Really. Feel better now? Good. Eat the *bing*. Hold it in your hands. Your hands . . . are beautiful. Lift it to your mouth. Your mouth . . . is beautiful. Bite it with your teeth. Your teeth . . . are beautiful. Crush it with your tongue. Your tongue . . . is beautiful. Slide it down your throat. Your throat . . . is beautiful.

STEVE: Our hands are beautiful.

(Grace holds hers next to his.)

GRACE: What do you see?

STEVE: I see . . . I see the hands of warriors.

GRACE: Warriors? What of gods, then?

STEVE: There are no gods that travel. Only warriors travel. *(Silence)* Would you like to go dance?

GRACE: Yeah. Okay. Sure.

(They start to leave. Dale speaks softly:)

DALE: Well, if you want to be alone . . .

GRACE: I think we would, Dale. Is that okay? *(Pause)* Thanks for coming over. I'm sorry things got so screwed up.

DALE: Oh—uh—that's okay. The evening was real . . . different, anyway.

GRACE: Yeah. Maybe you can take Frank off the tracks now?

DALE *(Laughing softly)*: Yeah. Maybe I will.

STEVE *(To Dale)*: Very nice meeting you. *(Extends his hand)*

DALE *(Does not take it)*: Yeah. Same here.

(Steve and Grace start to leave.)

You know . . . I think you picked up English faster than anyone I've ever met.

(Pause.)

STEVE: Thank you.

GRACE: See you.

STEVE: Good-bye.

DALE: 'Bye.

(Grace and Steve exit.)

Coda

Dale is alone in the back room. He examines the swords, the tablecloth, the box. He sits down.

DALE: F-O-B. Fresh Off the Boat, FOB. Clumsy, ugly, greasy FOB. Loud, stupid, four-eyed FOB. Big feet. Horny. Like Lenny in *Of Mice and Men.* F-O-B. Fresh Off the Boat. FOB.

(Slow fade to black.)

END OF PLAY

THE DANCE
AND THE
RAILROAD

(1981)

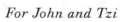

For John and Tzi

Production History

The Dance and the Railroad, commissioned by the New Federal Theatre under a grant from the U.S. Department of Education, opened at the New Federal Theatre (Woodie King, Jr., and Steve Tennen, Producers) in New York City on March 25, 1981. Special thanks for this production to Jack Tchen and the New York Chinatown History Project, and Genny Chomori of the UCLA Asian American Studies Center. It was directed by John Lone; the set sculpture was by Andrea Zakin, the costume design was by Judy Dearing; the lighting design was by Grant Orenstein; the music and choreography was by John Lone; and the production stage manager was Alice Jankowiak. The cast was as follows:

LONE   John Lone
MA   Tzi Ma

The Dance and the Railroad opened at The Joseph Papp Public Theater/New York Shakespeare Festival (Joseph Papp, Producer) in New York City, on July 16, 1981. It was directed by John Lone; the set design was by Karen Schulz; the costume design was by Judy Dearing; the lighting design was by Victor En Yu Tan; the music and choreography was by John Lone; and the production stage manager was Alice Jankowiak. The cast was as follows:

LONE   John Lone
MA   Tzi Ma

Characters

LONE, twenty years old, Chinaman railroad worker.
MA, eighteen years old, Chinaman railroad worker.

Place

A mountaintop near the transcontinental railroad.

Time

June 1867.

Scene One: afternoon.
Scene Two: afternoon, a day later.
Scene Three: late afternoon, four days later.
Scene Four: late that night.
Scene Five: just before the following dawn.

Definitions

die siu is a game of chance.
pi pa is a Chinese lute.

Scene One

A mountaintop. Afternoon. Lone is practicing Chinese opera steps. He swings his pigtail around like a fan. Ma enters, cautiously, watches from a hidden spot. Ma approaches Lone.

LONE: So, there are insects hiding in the bushes.
MA: Hey, listen, we haven't met, but—
LONE: I don't spend time with insects.

> *(Lone whips his hair into Ma's face; Ma backs off. Lone pursues him, swiping at Ma with his hair.)*

MA: What the—? Cut it out!
LONE: Don't push me.
MA: What was that for?
LONE: Don't ever push me again.
MA: You mess like that, you're gonna get pushed.
LONE: Don't push me.
MA: You started it. I just wanted to watch.
LONE: You "just wanted to watch." Did you ask my permission?
MA: What?
LONE: Did you?
MA: C'mon.
LONE: You can't expect to get in for free.
MA: Listen. I got some stuff you'll wanna hear.
LONE: You think so?
MA: Yeah. Some advice.
LONE: Advice? How old are you, anyway?
MA: Eighteen.

LONE: A child.

MA: Yeah. Right. A child. But listen—

LONE: A child who tries to advise a grown man—

MA: Listen, you got this kind of attitude.

LONE: —is a child who will never grow up.

MA: You know, the Chinamen down at camp, they can't stand it.

LONE: Oh?

MA: Yeah. You gotta watch yourself. You know what they say? They call you "Prince of the Mountain." Like you're too good to spend time with them.

LONE: Perceptive of them.

MA: After all, you never sing songs, never tell stories. They say you act like your spit is too clean for them, and they got ways to fix that.

LONE: Is that so?

MA: Like they're gonna bury you in the shit buckets, so you'll have more to clean than your nails.

LONE: But I don't shit.

MA: Or they're gonna cut out your tongue, since you never speak to them.

LONE: There's no one here worth talking to.

MA: Cut it out, Lone. Look, I'm trying to help you, all right? I got a solution.

LONE: So young yet so clever—

MA: That stuff you're doing—it's beautiful. Why don't you do it for the guys at camp? Help us celebrate?

LONE: What will "this stuff" help celebrate?

MA: C'mon. The strike, of course. Guys on a railroad gang, we gotta stick together, you know.

LONE: This is something to celebrate?

MA: Yeah. Yesterday, the weak-kneed Chinamen, they were running around like chickens without a head: "The white devils are sending their soldiers! Shoot us all!" But now, look—day four, see? Still in one piece. Those soldiers—we've never seen a gun or a bullet.

LONE: So you're all warrior-spirits, huh?

MA: They're scared of us, Lone—that's what it means.

LONE: I appreciate your advice. Tell you what—you go down—

MA: Yeah?

LONE: Down to the camp—

MA: Okay.

LONE: To where the men are—

MA: Yeah?

LONE: Sit there—

MA: Yeah?

LONE: And wait for me.

MA: Okay. *(Pause)* That's it? What do you think I am?

LONE: I think you're an insect interrupting my practice. So fly away. Go home.

MA: Look, I didn't come here to get laughed at.

LONE: No, I suppose you didn't.

MA: So just stay up here. By yourself. You deserve it.

LONE: I do.

MA: And don't expect any more help from me.

LONE: I haven't gotten any yet.

MA: If one day, you wake up and your head is buried in the shit can—

LONE: Yes?

MA: You can't find your body, your tongue is cut out—

LONE: Yes.

MA: Don't worry, 'cause I'll be there.

LONE: Oh.

MA: To make sure your mother's head is sitting right next to yours. *(He exits)*

LONE: His head is too big for this mountain. *(Returns to practicing)*

Scene Two

Mountaintop. Afternoon, the next day. Lone is practicing. Ma enters.

MA: Hey.

LONE: You? Again?

MA: I forgive you.

LONE: You . . . what?

MA: For making fun of me yesterday. I forgive you.

LONE: You can't—

MA: No. Don't thank me.

LONE: You can't forgive me.

MA: No. Don't mention it.

LONE: You—! I never asked for your forgiveness.

MA: I know. That's just the kinda guy I am.

LONE: This is ridiculous. Why don't you leave? Go down to your friends and play soldiers, sing songs, tell stories.

MA: Ah! See? That's just it. I got other ways I wanna spend my time. Will you teach me the opera?

LONE: What?

MA: I wanna learn it. I dreamt about it all last night.

LONE: No.

MA: The dance. The opera—I can do it.

LONE: You think so?

MA: Yeah. When I get outa here, I wanna go back to China and perform.

LONE: You want to become an actor?

MA: Well, I wanna perform.

LONE: Don't you remember the story about the three sons whose parents send them away to learn a trade? After three years, they return. The first one says, "I have become a coppersmith." The parents say, "Good. Second son, what have you become?" "I've become a silversmith." "Good—and youngest son, what about you?" "I have become an actor." When the parents hear that their son has become only an actor, they are very sad. The mother beats her head against the ground until the ground, out of pity, opens up and swallows her. The father is so angry he can't even speak, and the anger builds up inside him until it blows his body to pieces—little bits of his skin are found hanging from trees days later. You don't know how you endanger your relatives by becoming an actor.

MA: Well, I don't wanna become an "actor." That sounds terrible. I just wanna perform. Look, I'll be rich by the time I get out of here, right?

LONE: Oh?

MA: Sure. By the time I go back to China, I'll ride in gold sedan chairs, with twenty wives fanning me all around.

LONE: Twenty wives? This boy is ambitious.

MA: I'll give out pigs on New Year's and keep a stable of small birds to give to any woman who pleases me. And in my spare time, I'll perform.

LONE: Between your twenty wives and your birds, where will you find a free moment?

MA: I'll play Gwan Gung and tell stories of what life was like on the Gold Mountain.

LONE: Ma, just how long have you been in "America"?

MA: Huh? About four weeks.

LONE: You are a big dreamer.

MA: Well, all us Chinamen here are—right? Men with little dreams—have little brains to match. They walk with their eyes down, trying to find extra grains of rice on the ground.

LONE: So, you know all about "America"? Tell me, what kind of stories will you tell?

MA: I'll say, "We laid tracks like soldiers. Mountains? We hung from cliffs in baskets and the winds blew us like birds. Snow? We lived underground like moles for days at a time. Deserts? We—"

LONE: Wait. Wait. How do you know these things after only four weeks?

MA: They told me—the other Chinamen on the gang. We've been telling stories ever since the strike began.

LONE: They make it sound like it's very enjoyable.

MA: They said it is.

LONE: Oh? And you believe them?

MA: They're my friends. Living underground in winter—sounds exciting, huh?

LONE: Did they say anything about the cold?

MA: Oh, I already know about that. They told me about the mild winters and the warm snow.

LONE: Warm snow?

MA: When I go home, I'll bring some back to show my brothers.

LONE: Bring some—? On the boat?

MA: They'll be shocked—they've never seen American snow before.

LONE: You can't. By the time you get snow to the boat, it'll have melted, evaporated and returned as rain already.

MA: No.

LONE: No?

MA: Stupid.

LONE: Me?

MA: You been here awhile, haven't you?

LONE: Yes. Two years.

MA: Then how come you're so stupid? This is the Gold Mountain. The snow here doesn't melt. It's not wet.

LONE: That's what they told you?

MA: Yeah. It's true.

LONE: Did anyone show you any of this snow?

MA: No. It's not winter.

LONE: So where does it go?

MA: Huh?

LONE: Where does it go, if it doesn't melt? What happens to it?

MA: The snow? I dunno. I guess it just stays around.

LONE: So where is it? Do you see any?

MA: Here? Well, no, but . . . *(Pause)* This is probably one of those places where it doesn't snow—even in winter.

LONE: Oh.

MA: Anyway, what's the use of me telling you what you already know? Hey, c'mon—teach me some of that stuff. Look—I've been practicing the walk—how's this? *(Demonstrates)*

LONE: You look like a duck in heat.

MA: Hey—it's a start, isn't it?

LONE: Tell you what—you want to play some *die siu?*

MA: *Die siu?* Sure.

LONE: You know, I'm pretty good.

MA: Hey, I play with the guys at camp. You can't be any better than Lee—he's really got it down.

(Lone pulls out a case with two dice.)

LONE: I used to play 'til morning.

MA: Hey, us too. We see the sun start to rise, and say, "Hey,
if we go to sleep now, we'll never get up for work." So
we just keep playing.

LONE *(Holding out dice)*: *Die* or *siu?*

MA: *Siu.*

LONE: You sure?

MA: Yeah!

LONE: All right. *(He rolls) Die!*

MA: *Siu!*

(They see the result.)

Not bad.

*(They continue taking turns rolling throughout the fol-
lowing section; Ma always loses.)*

LONE: I haven't touched these in two years.

MA: I gotta practice more.

LONE: Have you lost much money?

MA: Huh? So what?

LONE: Oh, so you have gold hidden in all your shirt linings,
huh?

MA: Here in "America" —losing is no problem. You
know—End of the Year Bonus?

LONE: Oh, right.

MA: After I get that, I'll laugh at what I lost.

LONE: Lee told you there was a bonus, right?

MA: How'd you know?

LONE: When I arrived here, Lee told me there was a bonus, too.

MA: Lee teach you how to play?

LONE: Him? He talked to me a lot.

MA: Look, why don't you come down and start playing with the guys again?

LONE: "The guys."

MA: Before we start playing, Lee uses a stick to write "Kill!" in the dirt.

LONE: You seem to live for your nights with "the guys."

MA: What's life without friends, huh?

LONE: What?

MA: Hey, just kidding.

LONE: Who's getting killed here?

MA: Just a joke.

LONE: That's not a joke, it's blasphemy.

MA: Look, obviously you stopped playing 'cause you wanted to practice the opera.

LONE: Do you understand that discipline?

MA: But, I mean, you don't have to overdo either. You don't have to treat 'em like dirt. I mean, who are you trying to impress?

(Pause. Lone throws the dice into the bushes.)

LONE: Ooooops. Better go see who won.

MA: Hey! C'mon! Help me look!

LONE: If you find them, they are yours.

MA: You serious?

LONE: Yes.

(Ma finds the dice.)

MA: Here.

LONE: Who won?

MA: I didn't check.

LONE: Well, no matter. Keep the dice. Take them and go play with your friends.

MA: Here. *(He offers them to Lone)* A present.

LONE: A present? This isn't a present!

MA: They're mine, aren't they? You gave them to me, right?

LONE: Well, yes, but—

MA: So now I'm giving them to you.

LONE: You can't give me a present. I don't want them.

MA: You wanted them enough to keep them two years.

LONE: I'd forgotten I had them.

MA: See, I know, Lone. You wanna get rid of me. But you can't. I'm paying for lessons.

LONE: With my dice.

MA: Mine now. *(He offers them again)* Here.

(Pause. Lone runs Ma's hand across his forehead.)

LONE: Feel this.

MA: Hey!

LONE: Pretty wet, huh?

MA: Big deal.

LONE: Well, it's not from playing with *die siu.*

MA: I know how to sweat. I wouldn't be here if I didn't.

LONE: Yes, but are you willing to sweat after you've finished sweating? Are you willing to come up after you've spent the whole day chipping half an inch off a rock, and punish your body some more?

MA: Yeah. Even after work, I still—

LONE: No, you don't. You want to gamble, and tell dirty stories, and dress up like women to do shows.

MA: Hey, I never did that.

LONE: You've only been here a month. *(Pause)* And what about "the guys"? They're not going to treat you so well once you stop playing with them. Are you willing to work all day listening to them whisper, "That one— let's put spiders in his soup"?

MA: They won't do that to me. With you, it's different.

LONE: Is it?

MA: You don't have to act that way.

LONE: What way?

MA: Like you're so much better than them.

LONE: No. You haven't even begun to understand. To practice every day, you must have a fear to force you up
here.

MA: A fear? No—it's 'cause what you're doing is beautiful.

LONE: No.

MA: I've seen it.

LONE: It's ugly to practice when the mountain has turned
your muscles to ice. When my body hurts too much to
come here, I look at the other Chinamen and think,
"They are dead. Their muscles work only because the
white man forces them. I live because I can still force
my muscles to work for me." Say it. "They are dead."

MA: No. They're my friends.

LONE: Well, then take your dice down to your friends.

MA: But I want to learn—

LONE: This is your first lesson.

MA: Look, it shouldn't matter—

LONE: It does.

MA: It shouldn't matter what I think.

LONE: Attitude is everything.

MA: But as long as I come up, do the exercises—

LONE: I'm not going to waste time on a quitter.

MA: I'm not!

LONE: Then say it—"They are dead men."

MA: I can't.

LONE: Then you will never have the dedication.

MA: That doesn't prove anything.

LONE: I will not teach a dead man.

MA: What?

LONE: If you can't see it, then you're dead too.

MA: Don't start pinning—

LONE: Say it!

MA: All right.

LONE: What?

MA: All right. I'm one of them. I'm a dead man too.

(Pause.)

LONE: I thought as much. So, go. You have your friends.

MA: But I don't have a teacher.

LONE: I don't think you need both.

MA: Are you sure?

LONE: I'm being questioned by a child.

(Lone returns to practicing. Silence.)

MA: Look, Lone, I'll come up here every night—after work—I'll spend my time practicing, okay? *(Pause)* But I'm not gonna say that they're dead. Look at them. They're on strike; dead men don't go on strike, Lone. The white devils—they try and stick us with a ten-hour day. We want a return to eight hours and also a fourteen-dollar-a-month raise. I learned the demon English—listen: "Eight hour a day good for white man, all same good for Chinaman." These are the demands of live Chinamen, Lone. Dead men don't complain.

LONE: All right, this is something new. No one can judge the Chinamen 'til after the strike.

MA: They say we'll hold out for months if we have to. The smart men will live on what we've hoarded.

LONE: A Chinaman's mouth can swallow the earth. *(He takes the dice)* While the strike is on, I'll teach you.

MA: And afterwards?

LONE: Afterwards—we'll decide then whether these are dead or live men.

MA: When can we start?

LONE: We've already begun. Give me your hand.

Scene Three

Late afternoon, four days later. Lone and Ma are doing physical exercises.

MA: How long will it be before I can play Gwan Gung?

LONE: How long before a dog can play the violin?

MA: Old Ah Hong—have you heard him play the violin?

LONE: Yes. Now, he should take his violin and give it to a dog.

MA: I think he sounds okay.

LONE: I think he caused that avalanche last winter.

MA: He used to play weddings back home.

LONE: Ah Hong?

MA: That's what he said.

LONE: You probably heard wrong.

MA: No.

LONE: He probably said he played for funerals.

MA: He's been playing for the guys down at camp.

LONE: He should play for the white devils—that will end this stupid strike.

MA: Yang told me for sure—it'll be over by tomorrow.

LONE: Eight days already. And Yang doesn't know anything.

MA: He said they're already down to an eight-hour day and five-dollar raise at the bargaining sessions.

LONE: Yang eats too much opium.

MA: That doesn't mean he's wrong about this.

LONE: You can't trust him. One time—last year—he went around camp looking in everybody's eyes and saying, "Your nails are too long. They're hurting my eyes." This went on for a week. Finally, all the men clipped their nails, made a big pile, which they wrapped in leaves and gave to him. Yang used the nails to season his food—he put it in his soup, sprinkled it on his rice, and never said a word about it again. Now tell me—are you going to trust a man who eats other men's fingernails?

MA: Well, all I know is we won't go back to work until they meet all our demands. Listen, teach me some Gwan Gung steps.

LONE: I should have expected this. A boy who wants to have twenty wives is the type who demands more than he can handle.

MA: Just a few.

LONE: It takes years before an actor can play Gwan Gung.

MA: I can do it. I spend a lot of time watching the opera when it comes around. Every time I see Gwan Gung, I say, "Yeah. That's me. The god of fighters. The god of adventurers. We have the same kind of spirit."

LONE: I tell you, if you work very hard, when you return to China, you can perhaps be the Second Clown.

MA: Second Clown?

LONE: If you work hard.

MA: What's the Second Clown?

LONE: You can play the *pi pa*, and dance and jump all over.

MA: I'll buy them.

LONE: Excuse me?

MA: I'm going to be rich, remember? I'll buy a troupe and force them to let me play Gwan Gung.

LONE: I hope you have enough money, then, to pay audiences to sit through your show.

MA: You mean, I'm going to have to practice here every night—and in return, all I can play is the Second Clown?

LONE: If you work hard.

MA: Am I that bad? Maybe I shouldn't even try to do this. Maybe I should just go down.

LONE: It's not you. Everyone must earn the right to play Gwan Gung. I entered opera school when I was ten years old. My parents decided to sell me for ten years to this opera company. I lived with eighty other boys and we slept in bunks four beds high and hid our candy and rice cakes from each other. After eight years, I was studying to play Gwan Gung.

MA: Eight years?

LONE: I was one of the best in my class. One day, I was summoned by my master, who told me I was to go home for two days because my mother had fallen very ill and was dying. When I arrived home, Mother was standing at the door waiting, not sick at all. Her first words to me, the son away for eight years, were, "You've been playing while your village has starved. You must go to the Gold Mountain and work."

MA: And you never returned to school?

LONE: I went from a room with eighty boys to a ship with three hundred men. So, you see, it does not come easily to play Gwan Gung.

MA: Did you want to play Gwan Gung?

LONE: What a foolish question!

MA: Well, you're better off this way.

LONE: What?

MA: Actors—they don't make much money. Here, you make a bundle, then go back and be an actor again. Best of both worlds.

LONE: "Best of both worlds."

MA: Yeah!

(Lone drops to the ground, begins imitating a duck, waddling and quacking.)

Lone? What are you doing?

(Lone quacks.)

You're a duck?

(Lone quacks.)

I can see that.

(Lone quacks.)

Is this an exercise? Am I supposed to do this?

(Lone quacks.)

This is dumb. I never seen Gwan Gung waddle.

(Lone quacks.)

Okay. All right. I'll do it.

(Ma and Lone quack and waddle.)

You know, I never realized before how uncomfortable a duck's life is. And you have to listen to yourself quacking all day. Go crazy!

(Lone stands up straight.)

Now, what was all that about?

LONE: No, no. Stay down there, duck.

MA: What's the—

LONE *(Prompting)*: Quack, quack, quack.

MA: I don't—

LONE: Act your species!

MA: I'm not a duck!

LONE: Nothing worse than a duck that doesn't know his place.

MA: All right. *(Mechanically)* Quack, quack.

LONE: More.

MA: Quack.

LONE: More!

MA: Quack, quack, quack!

(Ma now continues quacking as Lone gives commands.)

LONE: Louder! It's your mating call! Think of your twenty duck wives! Good! Louder! Project! More! Don't slow down! Put your tail feathers into it! They can't hear you!

(Ma is now quacking up a storm. Lone exits, unnoticed by Ma.)

MA: Quack! Quack! Quack! Quack. Quack . . . quack. *(He looks around)* Quack . . . quack . . . Lone? . . . Lone? *(He waddles around the stage, looking for Lone)* Lone, where are you? Where'd you go? *(He stops, scratches his left leg with his right foot)* C'mon—stop playing around. What is this?

(Lone enters as a tiger, unseen by Ma.)

Look, let's call it a day, okay? I'm getting hungry.

(Ma turns around, notices Lone right before Lone is about to bite him.)

Aaaaah! Quack, quack, quack!

(They face off, in character as animals. Duck/Ma is terrified.)

LONE: Grrrr!
MA *(As a cry for help)*: Quack, quack, quack!

(Lone pounces on Ma. They struggle, in character. Ma is quacking madly, eyes tightly closed. Lone stands up straight. Ma continues to quack.)

LONE: Stand up.
MA *(Eyes still closed)*: Quack, quack, quack!
LONE *(Louder)*: Stand up!
MA *(Opening his eyes)*: Oh.
LONE: What are you?
MA: Huh?
LONE: A Chinaman or a duck?
MA: Huh? Gimme a second to remember.
LONE: You like being a duck?
MA: My feet fell asleep.
LONE: You change forms so easily.
MA: You said to.
LONE: What else could you turn into?
MA: Well, you scared me—sneaking up like that.
LONE: Perhaps a rock. That would be useful. When the men need to rest, they can sit on you.
MA: I got carried away.
LONE: Let's try . . . a locust. Can you become a locust?
MA: No. Let's cut this, okay?
LONE: Here. It's easy. You just have to know how to hop.
MA: You're not gonna get me—
LONE: Like this. *(He demonstrates)*
MA: Forget it, Lone.
LONE: I'm a locust. *(He begins jumping toward Ma)*

MA: Hey! Get away!

LONE: I devour whole fields.

MA: Stop it.

LONE: I starve babies before they are born.

MA: Hey, look, stop it!

LONE: I cause famines and destroy villages.

MA: I'm warning you! Get away!

LONE: What are you going to do? You can't kill a locust.

MA: You're not a locust.

LONE: You kill one, and another sits on your hand.

MA: Stop following me.

LONE: Locusts always trouble people, if not, we'd feel useless. Now, if you become a locust, too . . .

MA: I'm not going to become a locust.

LONE: Just stick your teeth out!

MA: I'm not gonna be a bug! It's stupid!

LONE: No man who's just been a duck has the right to call
anything stupid.

MA: I thought you were trying to teach me something.

LONE: I am. Go ahead.

MA: All right. There. That look right?

LONE: Your legs should be a little lower. Lower! There. That's
adequate. So how does it feel to be a locust? *(He gets up)*

MA: I dunno. How long do I have to do this?

LONE: Could you do it for three years?

MA: Three years? Don't be—

LONE: You couldn't, could you? Could you be a duck for that
long?

MA: Look, I wasn't born to be either of those.

LONE: Exactly. Well, I wasn't born to work on a railroad,
either. "Best of both worlds." How can you be such an
insect!

(Pause.)

MA: Lone . . .

LONE: Stay down there! Don't move! I've never told anyone
my story—the story of my parents' kidnapping me

from school. All the time we were crossing the ocean, the last two years here—I've kept my mouth shut. To you, I finally tell it. And all you can say is, "Best of both worlds." You're a bug to me, a locust. You think you understand the dedication one must have to be in the opera? You think it's the same as working on a railroad.

MA: Lone, all I was saying is that you'll go back too, and—

LONE: You're no longer a student of mine.

MA: What?

LONE: You have no dedication.

MA: Lone, I'm sorry.

LONE: Get up.

MA: I'm honored that you told me that.

LONE: Get up.

MA: No.

LONE: No?

MA: I don't want to. I want to talk.

LONE: Well, I've learned from the past. You're stubborn. You don't go. All right. Stay there. If you want to prove to me that you're dedicated, be a locust 'til morning. I'll go.

MA: Lone, I'm really honored that you told me.

LONE: I'll return in the morning. *(Exits)*

MA: Lone? Lone, that's ridiculous. You think I'm gonna stay like this? If you do, you're crazy. Lone? Come back here.

Scene Four

Late that night. Ma, alone, still in locust position.

MA: Locusts travel in huge swarms, so large that when they cross the sky, they block out the sun, like a storm. Second Uncle—back home—when he was a young man, his whole crop got wiped out by locusts one year.

In the famine that followed, Second Uncle lost his eldest son and his second wife—the one he married for love. Even to this day, we look around before saying the word "locust," to make sure Second Uncle is out of hearing range. About eight years ago, my brother and I discovered Second Uncle's cave in back of the stream near our house. We saw him come out of it one day around noon. Later, just before the sun went down, we sneaked in. We only looked once. Inside, there must have been hundreds—maybe five hundred or more—grasshoppers in huge bamboo cages—and around them—stacks of grasshopper legs, grasshopper heads, grasshopper antennae, grasshoppers with one leg, still trying to hop but toppling like trees coughing, grasshoppers wrapped around sharp branches rolling from side to side, grasshoppers' legs cut off grasshopper bodies, then tied around grasshoppers and tightened 'til grasshoppers died. Every conceivable kind of grasshopper in every conceivable stage of life and death, subject to every conceivable grasshopper torture. We ran out quickly, my brother and I—we knew an evil place by the thickness of the air. Now, I think of Second Uncle. How sad that the locusts forced him to take out his agony on innocent grasshoppers. What if Second Uncle could see me now? Would he cut off my legs? He might as well. I can barely feel them. But then again, Second Uncle never tortured actual locusts, just weak grasshoppers.

Scene Five

Just before dawn. Ma is still in locust position.

LONE *(Offstage, singing)*:
Hit your hardest
Pound out your tears

> The more you try
> The more you'll cry
> At how little I've moved
> And how large I loom
> By the time the sun goes down

MA: You look rested.

LONE: Me?

MA: Well, you sound rested.

LONE: No, not at all.

MA: Maybe I'm just comparing you to me.

LONE: I didn't even close my eyes all last night.

MA: Aw, Lone, you didn't have to stay up for me. You coulda just come up here and—

LONE: For you?

MA: —apologized and everything woulda been—

LONE: I didn't stay up for you.

MA: Huh? You didn't?

LONE: No.

MA: Oh. You sure?

LONE: Positive. I was thinking, that's all.

MA: About me?

LONE: Well . . .

MA: Even a little?

LONE: I was thinking about the Chinamen—and you. Get up, Ma.

MA: Aw, do I have to? I've gotten to know the grasshoppers real well.

LONE: Get up. I have a lot to tell you.

MA: What'll they think? They take me in, even though I'm a little large, then they find out I'm a human being. I stepped on their kids. No trust. Gimme a hand, will you?

(Lone helps Ma up, but Ma's legs can't support him.)

Aw, shit. My legs are coming off. *(He lies down and tries to straighten his legs out)*

LONE: I have many surprises. First, you will play Gwan Gung.

MA: My legs will be sent home without me. What'll my family think? Come to port to meet me and all they get is two legs.

LONE: Did you hear me?

MA: Hold on. I can't be in agony and listen to Chinese at the same time.

LONE: Did you hear my first surprise?

MA: No. I'm too busy screaming.

LONE: I said, you'll play Gwan Gung.

MA: Gwan Gung?

LONE: Yes.

MA: Me?

LONE: Yes.

MA: Without legs?

LONE: What?

MA: That might be good.

LONE: Stop that!

MA: I'll become a legend. Like the blind man who defended Amoy.

LONE: Did you hear?

MA: "The legless man who played Gwan Gung."

LONE: Isn't this what you want? To play Gwan Gung?

MA: No, I just wanna sleep.

LONE: No, you don't. Look. Here I brought you something.

MA: Food?

LONE: Here. Some rice.

MA: Thanks, Lone. And duck?

LONE: Just a little.

MA: Where'd you get the duck?

LONE: Just bones and skin.

MA: We don't have duck. And the white devils have been blockading the food.

LONE: Sing—he had some left over.

MA: Sing? That thief?

LONE: And something to go with it.

MA: What? Lone, where did you find whiskey?

LONE: You know, Sing—he has almost anything.

MA: Yeah. For a price.

LONE: Once, even some thousand-day-old eggs.

MA: He's a thief. That's what they told me.

LONE: Not if you're his friend.

MA: Sing don't have any real friends. Everyone talks about him bein' tied in to the head of the klan in San Francisco. Lone, you didn't have to do this. Here. Have some.

LONE: I had plenty.

MA: Don't gimme that. This cost you plenty, Lone.

LONE: Well, I thought if we were going to celebrate, we should do it as well as we would have at home.

MA: Celebrate? What for? Wait.

LONE: Ma, the strike is over.

MA: Shit, I knew it. And we won, right?

LONE: Yes, the Chinamen have won. They can do more than just talk.

MA: I told you. Didn't I tell you?

LONE: Yes. Yes, you did.

MA: Yang told me it was gonna be done. He said—

LONE: Yes, I remember.

MA: Didn't I tell you? Huh?

LONE: Ma, eat your duck.

MA: Nine days, we civilized the white devils. I knew it. I knew we'd hold out 'til their ears started twitching. So that's where you got the duck, right? At the celebration?

LONE: No, there wasn't a celebration.

MA: Huh? You sure? Chinamen—they look for any excuse to party.

LONE: But I thought *we* should celebrate.

MA: Well, that's for sure.

LONE: So you will play Gwan Gung.

MA: God, nine days. Shit, it's finally done. Well, we'll show them how to party. Make noise. Jump off rocks. Make the mountain shake.

LONE: We'll wash your body, to prepare you for the role.

MA: What role?

LONE: Gwan Gung. I've been telling you.

MA: I don't wanna play Gwan Gung.

LONE: You've shown the dedication required to become my student, so—

MA: Lone, you think I stayed up last night 'cause I wanted to play Gwan Gung?

LONE: You said you were like him.

MA: I am. Gwan Gung stayed up all night once to prove his loyalty. Well, now I have too. Lone, I'm honored that you told me your story.

LONE: Yes . . . That is like Gwan Gung.

MA: Good. So let's do an opera about *me*.

LONE: What?

MA: You wanna party or what?

LONE: About you?

MA: You said I was like Gwan Gung, didn't you?

LONE: Yes, but—

MA: Well, look at the operas he's got. I ain't even got one.

LONE: Still, you can't—

MA: You tell me, is that fair?

LONE: You can't do an opera about yourself.

MA: I just won a victory, didn't I? I deserve an opera in my honor.

LONE: But it's not traditional.

MA: Traditional? Lone, you gotta figure any way I could do Gwan Gung wasn't gonna be traditional anyway. I may be as good a guy as him, but he's a better dancer. *(Sings)*

Old Gwan Gung, just sits about
'Til the dime-store fighters have had it out
Then he pitches his peach pit
Combs his beard
Draws his sword
And they scatter in fear

LONE: What are you talking about?

MA: I just won a great victory. I get—whatcha call it?— poetic license. C'mon. Hit the gongs. I'll immortalize my story.

LONE: I refuse. This goes against all my training. I try and give you your wish and—

MA: Do it. Gimme my wish. Hit the gongs.

LONE: I never—I can't.

MA: Can't what? Don't think I'm worth an opera? No, I guess not. I forgot—you think I'm just one of those dead men.

(Silence. Lone pulls out a gong. Ma gets into position to begin. Lone hits the gong. They do the following in mock-Chinese-opera style.)

I am Ma. Yesterday, I was kicked out of my house by my three elder brothers, calling me the lazy dreamer of the family. I am sitting here in front of the temple trying to decide how I will avenge this indignity. Here comes the poorest beggar in this village. *(He cues Lone)* He is called Fleaman because his body is the most popular meeting place for fleas from around the province.

LONE *(Singing)*:
Fleas in love,
Find your happiness
In the gray scraps of my suit

MA: Hello, Flea—

LONE *(Continuing)*:
Fleas in need
Shield your families
In the gray hairs of my beard

MA: Hello, Flea—

(Lone cuts Ma off, continues an extended improvised aria.)

Hello, Fleaman.

LONE: Hello, Ma. Are you interested in providing a home for these fleas?

MA: No!

LONE: This couple here—seeking to start a new home. Housing today is so hard to find. How about your left arm?

MA: I may have plenty of my own fleas in time. I have been thrown out by my elder brothers.

LONE: Are you seeking revenge? A flea epidemic on your house? *(To a flea)* Get back there. You should be asleep. Your mother will worry.

MA: Nothing would make my brothers angrier than seeing me rich.

LONE: Rich? After the bad crops of the last three years, even the fleas are thinking of moving north.

MA: I heard a white devil talk yesterday.

LONE: Oh—with hair the color of a sick chicken and eyes round as eggs? The fleas and I call him Chicken-Laying-an-Egg.

MA: He said we can make our fortunes on the Gold Mountain, where work is play and the sun scares off snow.

LONE: Don't listen to chicken-brains.

MA: Why not? He said gold grows like weeds.

LONE: I have heard that it is slavery.

MA: Slavery? What do you know, Fleaman? Who told you? The fleas? Yes, I will go to Gold Mountain.

(Sound of gongs. Ma strikes a submissive pose to Lone.)

LONE: "The one-hundred-twenty-five-dollars passage money is to be paid to the said head of said Hong, who will make arrangements with the coolies that their wages shall be deducted until the debt is absorbed."

(Ma bows to Lone. Sound of gongs. They pick up fighting sticks and do a water-crossing dance, using their sticks to imitate oars. Dance ends. They stoop next to each other and rock.)

MA: I have been in the bottom of this boat for thirty-six days now. Tang, how many have died?

LONE: Not me. I'll live through this ride.

MA: I didn't ask how you are.

LONE: But why's the Gold Mountain so far?

MA: We left with three hundred and three.

LONE: My family's depending on me.

MA: So tell me, how many have died?

LONE: I'll be the last one alive.

MA: That's not what I wanted to know.

LONE: I'll find some fresh air in this hole.

MA: I asked, how many have died.

LONE: Is that a crack in the side?

MA: Are you listening to me?

LONE: If I had some air—

MA: I asked, don't you see—?

LONE: The crack—over there—

MA: Will you answer me, please?

LONE: I need to get out.

MA: The rest here agree—

LONE: I can't stand the smell.

MA: That a hundred eighty—

LONE: I can't see the air—

MA: Of us will not see—

LONE: And I can't die.

MA: Our Gold Mountain dream.

> (*Tang/Lone dies. Using the movement language of Chinese opera, they mime the following: Ma throws his body overboard. The boat docks. Ma exits, walks through the streets. He picks up one of the fighting sticks while Lone becomes the mountain.*)

I have been given my pickax. Now I will attack the mountain.

> (*Ma does a dance of labor. Lone sings:*)

LONE:
    Hit your hardest
    Pound out your tears
    The more you try

The more you'll cry
At how little I've moved
And how large I loom
By the time the sun goes down

(Ma stops dancing.)

MA: This mountain is clever. But why shouldn't it be? It's fighting for its life, like we fight for ours.

(Lone/Mountain picks up a stick. Ma and Lone/Mountain do a battle dance. Dance ends.)

This mountain not only defends itself—it also attacks. It turns our strength against us.

(Lone does Ma's labor dance while Ma plants explosives in midair. Dance ends.)

This mountain has survived for millions of years. Its wisdom is immense.

(Lone and Ma begin a second battle dance. This one ends with them dancing together: Ma has subdued the mountain. Lone breaks away, does a warrior strut.)

LONE: I am a white devil! Listen to my stupid language: "Wha che doo doo blah blah." Look at my wide eyes— like I have drunk seventy-two pots of tea. Look at my funny hair—twisting, turning, like a snake telling lies. *(To Ma)* Blah blah doo doo tee tee.
MA: We don't understand English.
LONE *(Angry)*: Blah blah doo doo tee tee!
MA *(With Chinese accent)*: Please you-ah speak-ah Chinese?
LONE: Oh. Work—uh—one—two—more—work—two—
MA: Two hours more? Stupid demons. As confused as your hair. We will strike!

(Sound of gongs. Ma is on strike.)

(In broken English) Eight hours day good for white man, all same good for Chinaman.

LONE: The strike is over! We've won!

MA: I knew we would.

LONE: We forced the white devil to act civilized.

MA: Tamed the barbarians!

LONE: Did you think—

MA: Who woulda thought?

LONE: —it could be done?

MA: Who?

LONE: But who?

MA: Who could tame them?

MA AND LONE: Only a Chinaman!

(They laugh.)

LONE: Well, c'mon.

MA: Let's celebrate!

LONE: We have.

MA: Oh.

LONE: Back to work.

MA: But we've won the strike.

LONE: I know. Congratulations! And now—

MA: —back to work?

LONE: Right.

MA: No.

LONE: But the strike is over.

(Lone tosses Ma a stick. They resume their stick battle as before, but Ma is heard over Lone's singing.)

LONE:	MA:
Hit your hardest	Wait.
Pound out your tears	I'm tired of this!
	How do we end it?
The more you try	Let's stop now, all
The more you'll cry	right?
At how little I've moved	Look, I said enough!
And how large I loom	
By the time the sun goes down.	

84

(Ma tosses his stick away. Lone, already aiming a blow toward Ma's stick, hits Ma instead and mistakenly knocks him down.)

MA: Oh! Shit! . . .

LONE: I'm sorry! Are you all right?

MA: Yeah. I guess.

LONE: Why'd you let go? You can't just do that.

MA: I'm bleeding.

LONE: That was stupid—where?

MA: Here.

LONE: No.

MA: Ow!

LONE: There will probably be a bump.

MA: I dunno.

LONE: What?

MA: I dunno why I let go.

LONE: It was stupid.

MA: But how were we going to end the opera?

LONE: Here. *(He applies whiskey to Ma's bruise)* I don't know.

MA: Why didn't we just end it with the celebration? Ow! Careful.

LONE: Sorry. But Ma, the celebration's not the end. We're returning to work. Today. At dawn.

MA: What?

LONE: We've already lost nine days of work. But we got eight hours.

MA: Today? That's terrible.

LONE: What do you think we're here for? But they listened to our demands. We're getting a raise.

MA: Right. Fourteen dollars.

LONE: No. Eight.

MA: What?

LONE: We had to compromise. We got an eight-dollar raise.

MA: But we wanted fourteen. Why didn't we get fourteen?

LONE: It was the best deal they could get. Congratulations.

MA: Congratulations? Look, Lone, I'm sick of you making fun of the Chinamen.

LONE: Ma, I'm not. For the first time. I was wrong. We got eight dollars.

MA: We wanted fourteen.

LONE: But we got eight hours.

MA: We'll go back on strike.

LONE: Why?

MA: We could hold out for months.

LONE: And lose all that work?

MA: But we just gave in.

LONE: You're being ridiculous. We got eight hours. Besides, it's already been decided.

MA: I didn't decide. I wasn't there. You made me stay up here.

LONE: The heads of the gangs decide.

MA: And that's it?

LONE: It's done.

MA: Back to work? That's what they decided? Lone, I don't want to go back to work.

LONE: Who does?

MA: I forgot what it's like.

LONE: You'll pick up the technique again soon enough.

MA: I mean, what it's like to have them telling you what to do all the time. Using up your strength.

LONE: I thought you said even after work, you still feel good.

MA: Some days. But others . . . *(Pause)* I get so frustrated sometimes. At the rock. The rock doesn't give in. It's not human. I wanna claw it with my fingers, but that would just rip them up. I wanna throw myself head-first onto it, but it'd just knock my skull open. The rock would knock my skull open, then just sit there, still, like nothing had happened, like a faceless Buddha. *(Pause)* Lone, when do I get out of here?

LONE: Well, the railroad may get finished—

MA: It'll never get finished.

LONE: —or you may get rich.

MA: Rich. Right. This is the Gold Mountain. *(Pause)* Lone, has anyone ever gone home rich from here?

LONE: Yes. Some.

MA: But most?

LONE: Most . . . do go home.

MA: Do you still have the fear?

LONE: The fear?

MA: That you'll become like them—dead men?

LONE: Maybe I was wrong about them.

MA: Well, I do. You wanted me to say it before. I can say it now: "They are dead men." Their greatest accomplishment was to win a strike that's gotten us nothing.

LONE: They're sending money home.

MA: No.

LONE: It's not much. I know, but it's something.

MA: Lone, I'm not even doing that. If I don't get rich here, I might as well die here. Let my brothers laugh in peace.

LONE: Ma, you're too soft to get rich here, naive—you believed the snow was warm.

MA: I've got to change myself. Toughen up. Take no shit. Count my change. Learn to gamble. Learn to win. Learn to stare. Learn to deny. Learn to look at men with opaque eyes.

LONE: You want to do that?

MA: I will. 'Cause I've got the fear. You've given it to me.

(Pause.)

LONE: Will I see you here tonight?

MA: Tonight?

LONE: I just thought I'd ask.

MA: I'm sorry, Lone. I haven't got time to be the Second Clown.

LONE: I thought you might not.

MA: Sorry.

LONE: You could have been a . . . fair actor.

MA: You coming down? I gotta get ready for work. This is gonna be a terrible day. My legs are sore and my arms are outa practice.

LONE: You go first. I'm going to practice some before work. There's still time.

MA: Practice? But you said you lost your fear. And you said that's what brings you up here.

LONE: I guess I was wrong about that, too. Today, I am dancing for no reason at all.

MA: Do whatever you want. See you down at camp.

LONE: Could you do me a favor?

MA: A favor?

LONE: Could you take this down so I don't have to take it all? *(He points to a pile of props)*

MA: Well, okay. *(Pause)* But this is the last time.

LONE: Of course, Ma.

(Ma exits.)

See you soon. The last time. I suppose so.

(Lone resumes practicing. He twirls his hair around as in the beginning of the play. The sun begins to rise. It continues rising until Lone, moving, is seen only in shadow.)

END OF PLAY

FAMILY

DEVOTIONS

(1981)

For my Ama and Ankong,
and Sam Shepard

Production History

Family Devotions opened at The Joseph Papp Public
Theater/New York Shakespeare Festival (Joseph Papp,
Producer), in New York City on October 18, 1981. It was
directed by Robert Allan Ackerman; the set design was by
David Gropman; the costume design was by Willa Kim
and the lighting design was by Tom Skelton. The cast was as
follows:

JOANNE	Jodi Long
WILBUR	Jim Ishida
JENNY	Lauren Tom
AMA	Tina Chen
POPO	June Kim
HANNAH	Helen Funai
ROBERT	Michael Paul Chan
DI-GOU	Victor Wong
CHESTER	Marc Hayashi

Characters

JOANNE, Chinese-American raised in the Philippines, late thirties.

WILBUR, Joanne's husband, Japanese-American, *nisei* (second generation), late thirties.

JENNY, Joanne and Wilbur's daughter, seventeen.

AMA, Joanne's mother, born in China, emigrated to the Philippines, then to America.

POPO, Ama's younger sister.

HANNAH, Popo's daughter and Joanne's cousin, five years older than Joanne.

ROBERT, Hannah's husband, Chinese-American, first generation.

DI-GOU, Ama and Popo's younger brother, born and raised in China, still a resident of the People's Republic of China (P.R.C.).

CHESTER, Hannah and Robert's son, early twenties.

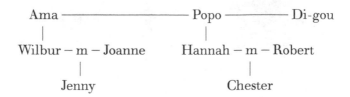

Place

The lanai/sunroom and tennis court of a home in Bel Air, California.

Time

1980.

Act I: late afternoon.
Act II: same scene, immediately following.

Definitions

bao is a steamed meat bun.
gao sai is dog dung.
guo-tieh is a fried meat dumpling.
jok is a Chinese rice porridge.

ACT I

As the curtain rises, we see a single spotlight on an old Chinese face and hear Chinese music or chanting. Suddenly, the music becomes modern-day funk or rock 'n' roll, and the lights come up to reveal the set: the lanai/sunroom and back-yard of a home in Bel Air. The sunroom has a glass roof and glass walls. Upstage of the lanai/sunroom is a patio with a barbecue and a tennis court. The tennis court leads offstage.

The face is that of Di-gou, an older Chinese man wear-ing a blue suit and carrying an old suitcase. He is standing on the tennis court and peering into the sunroom through the glass walls. Behind him, a stream of black smoke is coming from the barbecue.

JOANNE *(Offstage)*: Wilbur! Wilbur!

(Di-gou exits off the tennis court. Joanne enters from the house. She is a Chinese-American woman, attractive, in her late thirties. She sees the smoke coming from the bar-becue.)

Aiii-ya! *(She heads for the barbecue; on her way, she notices that the sunroom is a mess)* Jenny!

(She runs out to the barbecue, opens it up. Billows of black smoke continue to pour out.)

Oh, gosh. Oh, golly. *(To offstage)* Wilbur! *(She begins pulling burnt objects out of the barbecue)* Sheee! *(She pulls out a chicken, dumps it onto the ground)* Wilbur! *(She pulls out another chicken, does the same)* Wilbur, the heat was too high on the barbecue! *(She begins pulling out burnt objects and tossing them all over the tennis court)* You should have been watching it! It could have exploded! We could all have been blown up! *(She picks up another chicken, examines it)* You think we can save some of this? *(She pauses, tosses it onto the court)* We'll get some more chickens. We'll put barbecue sauce on them and stick them into the microwave. *(She exits into the house holding a chicken on the end of a fork)* Is this okay, do you think?

(Wilbur appears on the tennis court. He is a Japanese-American man, nisei *[second generation], in his late thirties. His hair is permed. He wears tennis clothes.)*

WILBUR: Hon? *(He looks around)* What's up? *(He picks a burnt chicken off the tennis court)* Hon? *(He walks over to the barbecue)* Who—? Why's the heat off? *(He walks around the tennis court picking up chickens)* Jesus! *(He smears grease on his white tennis shirt, then notices it)* Aw, shit! *(He dumps all the chickens except one, which he has forgotten to pick up, back into the barbecue. He walks into the sunroom, gets some ice and tries to dab at the stain)* Hon? Will you come here a sec? *(He exits into the house)*

(Jenny appears on the tennis court. She is seventeen, Wilbur and Joanne's daughter. She carries a large wire-mesh box.)

JENNY: Chickie! *(Looking around)* Chickie? Chickie, where the hell did you go? You know, it's embarrassing. It's embarrassing being this old and still having to chase a chicken all over the house. *(She sees the lone burnt chicken on the court. She creeps over slowly, then picks it up)* Blaagh! Who cooked this? See, Chickie, this is what happens—what happens when you're a bad chickie.

(Chester, a young Chinese-American male in his early twenties, appears on the tennis court. He tries to sneak up on Jenny.)

(To chicken) Look, if you bother Popo and Ama, I'm gonna catch shit, and you know what that means for you—chicken soccer. You'll be sorry.

(Chester is right behind Jenny.)

You'll be sorry if you mess with me.

(Jenny turns around, catching Chester.)

Oh, good. You have to be here, too.

CHESTER: No, I don't. I've gotta pack.

JENNY: They'll expect you to be here when that Chinese guy gets here. What's his name? Dar-gwo?

CHESTER: I dunno. Dah-gim?

JENNY: Doo-goo? Something.

CHESTER: Yeah. I'm not staying.

JENNY: So what else is new?

CHESTER: I don't have time.

JENNY: You luck out 'cause you don't live here. Me— there's no way I can get away. When you leaving?

CHESTER: Tomorrow.

JENNY: Tomorrow? And you're not packed?

CHESTER: Don't rub it in. Listen, you still have my green suitcase?

JENNY: Yeah. I wish *I* had an excuse not to be here. All I need is to meet another old relative. Another goon.

CHESTER: Yeah. Where's my suitcase?

JENNY: First you have to help me find Chickie.

CHESTER: Jesus!

AMA *(Offstage)*: Joanne!

CHESTER *(To Jenny)*: All right. I don't want them to know I'm here.

(Chester and Jenny exit. Popo, Joanne's aunt, and Ama, Joanne's mother, enter.)

AMA: Joanne! Joanne! Jenny! Where is Joanne?

POPO: Probably busy.

AMA: Where is Jenny? Joanne?

POPO: Perhaps you can find, ah, Wilbur.

AMA: Joanne!

POPO: Ah, you never wish to see Wilbur.

AMA: I see him at wedding. That is enough. He was not at church again today.

POPO: Ah?

AMA: He will be bad influence when Di-gou arrive. Wilbur—holy spirit is not in him.

POPO: Not matter. He can perhaps eat in kitchen.

AMA: Outside!

POPO: This is his house.

AMA: All heart must join as one—

POPO: He may eat inside!

AMA: —only then, miracles can take place.

POPO: But in kitchen

AMA: Wilbur—he never like family devotions.

POPO: Wilbur does not come from Christian family.

AMA: He come from Japanese family.

POPO: I mean to say, we—ah—very fortunate. Mama teach us all Christianity. Not like Wilbur family.

AMA: When Di-gou arrive, we will remind him. What Mama tells us.

POPO: Di-gou can remember himself.

AMA: No.

POPO: But we remember.

AMA: You forget—Di-gou, he lives in China.

POPO: So?

AMA: Torture. Communists. Make him work in rice fields.

POPO: I no longer think so.

AMA: In rice field, all the people wear wires in their heads— yes! Wires force them work all day and sing Communist song. Like this! *(She mimes harvesting rice and singing)*

POPO: No such thing!

AMA: Yes! You remember Twa-Ling? Before we leave China, before Communist come, she say, "I will send you a picture. If Communists are good, I will stand— if bad, I will sit."

POPO: That does not mean anything!

AMA: In picture she sent, she was lying down!

POPO: Picture was not sent for ten years. Probably she forget.

AMA: You wait 'til Di-gou arrive. You will see.

POPO: See what?

AMA: Brainwash! You watch for little bit of wires in his hair.

(Popo notices the lone burnt chicken on the tennis court.)

POPO: What's there?

AMA: Where?

POPO: There—on cement.

AMA: Cannot see well.

POPO: There. Black.

AMA: Oh. I see.

POPO: Looks like *gao sai.*

AMA: They sometimes have problem with the dog.

POPO: Ha!

AMA: Very bad dog.

POPO: At home, dog do that?—we shoot him.

AMA: Should be punish.

POPO: Shot! *(Pause)* That no *gao sai.*

AMA: No? What then?

POPO: I don't know.

AMA: Oh, I know.

POPO: What?

AMA: That is Chickie.

POPO. No. That no chickie.

AMA: They have a chicken—"Chickie."

(They get up, head toward the chicken.)

POPO: No. That one, does not move.

AMA: Maybe sick.

(They reach the chicken.)

Aiii-ya! What happen to Chickie!

POPO *(Picking it up)*: This chicken very sick! *(She laughs)*

AMA: Wilbur.

POPO: Huh?

AMA: Wilbur—his temper is very bad.

POPO: No!

AMA: Yes. Perhaps Chickie bother him too much.

POPO: No—this is only a chicken.

AMA: "Chickie" *is* chicken!

POPO: No—this—another chicken.

AMA: How you know?

POPO: No matter now. Like this, all chicken look same. Here. Throw away. No good.

AMA: Very bad temper. Japanese man.

(Ama sees Popo looking for a trash can.)

Wait.

POPO: Huh?

AMA: Jenny—might want to keep it.

POPO: This?

AMA: Leave here until we know. *(She takes the chicken from Popo)*

POPO: No, throw away. *(She takes it back)* Stink up whole place soon.

AMA: Don't want to anger Wilbur!

POPO: You pig-head!

AMA: He do this to Chickie—think what he will do to us?

POPO: *Zin gao tza!* [Always so much trouble!]

AMA: You don't know Japanese man!

(Ama knocks the chicken from Popo's hands; they circle around it like boxers sparring.)

POPO: *Pah-di!* [Spank you!]

AMA: Remember? During war? Pictures they show us? Always—Japanese man kill Chinese!

POPO: Go away, pig-head!

AMA: In picture—Japanese always kill and laugh, kill and laugh.

POPO: If dirty, should throw away!

AMA: Sometimes—torture and laugh, too.

POPO: Wilbur not like that! Hardly even laugh!

AMA: When he kill Chickie, then he laugh!

(They both grab the chicken; Joanne enters, sees them.)

JOANNE: Hi, Mom, Auntie. Who cleaned up the chicken?

AMA: Huh? This is not Chickie?

POPO *(To Ama)*: Tell you things, you never listen. *Gong-gong-ah!* [Idiot!]

JOANNE: When's Hannah getting here?

POPO: Hannah—she is at airport.

JOANNE: We had a little accident and I need help program-ming the microwave. Last time, I put a roast inside and it disintegrated. She should be here already.

AMA: Joanne, you prepare for family devotions?

JOANNE: Of course, Mom. I had the maid set up everything just like you said. *(She exits)*

AMA: Good. Praise to God will bring Di-gou back to family. Make him rid of Communist demon.

POPO: He will speak in tongue of fire. Like he does when he is a little boy with See-goh-poh.

(Wilbur enters the tennis court with an empty laundry basket. He heads for the barbecue. Joanne follows him.)

JOANNE *(To Wilbur)*: Hon, what are you going to do with those?

WILBUR *(Referring to the burnt chicken)*: I'm just going to give them to Grizzly. *(He piles the chickens into the basket)*

JOANNE: All right. *(She notices that the mess in the lanai has not been touched)* Jenny! *(To Wilbur)* But be careful not to give Grizzly any bones! *(She exits)*

WILBUR *(To Ama and Popo)*: How you doin', Mom, Auntie?

AMA *(To Popo, sotto voce)*: Kill and laugh.

WILBUR: Joanne tells me you're pretty excited about your brother's arrival—pretty understandable, after all these years—what's his name again? Di-ger, Di-gow, something . . .

AMA: Di-gou!

WILBUR: Yeah, right. Gotta remember that. Be pretty embarrassing if I said the wrong name. Di-gou.

POPO: Di-gou is not his name.

WILBUR: What? Not his—? What is it again? Di-gow? De—?

AMA: Di-gou!

POPO: That is not his name.

WILBUR: Oh. It's the tones in Chinese, isn't it? I'm saying the wrong tone: Di-gou? Or Di-gou? Or—

POPO: Di-gou meaning is "second brother."

WILBUR: Oh, I see. It's not his name. Boy, do I feel ignorant in these situations. If only there were some way I could make sure I don't embarrass myself tonight.

AMA: Eat outside.

WILBUR: Outside?

POPO: Or in kitchen.

WILBUR: In the kitchen? That's great! You two are real jokers, you know?

AMA: No. We are not.

WILBUR: C'mon. I should bring you down to the club someday. The guys never believe it when I tell them how much I love you two.

AMA *(To Popo)*: *Gao sai.*

(Jenny enters the sunroom.)

WILBUR: Right. "*Gao sai*" to you, too. *(He starts to leave, sees Jenny)* Wash your hands before you play with your grandmother.

JENNY *(To Wilbur)*: Okay, Dad. *(To Ama)* Do I have to, Ama?

AMA: No. Of course not.

JENNY: Can I ask you something personal?

AMA: Of course.

JENNY: Did Daddy just call you "dog shit"?

AMA: Jenny!

POPO: Yes. Very good!

JENNY: Doesn't that bother you?

POPO *(To Ama)*: Her Chinese is improving!

JENNY: We learned it in Chinese school.

AMA: Jenny, you should not use this American word.

JENNY: Sorry. It just slipped out.

AMA: You do not use such word at school, no?

JENNY: Oh, no. Of course not.

AMA: You should not use anyplace.

JENNY: Right.

POPO: Otherwise—no good man wants marry you.

JENNY: You mean, no rich man.

AMA: No—money is not important.

POPO: As long as he is good man.

(*Pause.*)

AMA: Christian.

POPO: Chinese.

AMA: Good education.

POPO: Good school.

AMA: Princeton.

POPO: Harvard.

AMA: Doctor.

POPO: Surgeon.

AMA: Brain surgeon.

POPO: Surgeon general.

AMA: Otherwise—you marry anyone that you like.

JENNY: Ama, Popo—look, I'm only seventeen.

POPO: True. But you can develop the good habits now.

JENNY: I don't want to get married till I'm at least thirty or something.

POPO: Thirty! By that time we are dead!

AMA: Gone to see God!

POPO: Lie in ground, arms cross!

JENNY: Look at it this way: how can I be a good mother if I have to follow my career around?

AMA: Your career will not require this.

JENNY: Yeah, it will. What if I have to go on tour?

AMA: Dental technicians do not tour.

JENNY: Ama!

POPO: Only tour—one mouth to next mouth: "Hello. Clean your teeth?"

JENNY: Look, I'm telling you, I'm going to be a dancer.

AMA: We say—you can do both. Combine skills.

JENNY: That's ridiculous.

POPO: Be first dancing dental technician.

JENNY: I don't wanna be a dental technician!

POPO: Dancing dental technician very rare. You will be very popular.

JENNY: Why can't I be like Chester?

AMA: You cannot be like Chester.

JENNY: Why not!

POPO: You do not play violin. Chester does not dance. No hope.

JENNY: I know, but, I mean, he's a musician. Why can't I be a dancer?

AMA: Chester—his work very dangerous.

JENNY: Dangerous?

AMA: He just receive new job—play with Boston Symphony.

JENNY: Yeah. I know. He's leaving tomorrow. So? What's so bad about Boston?

AMA: Conductor—Ozawa—he is Japanese.

JENNY: Oh no. Not this again.

AMA: Very strict. If musicians miss one note, they must kill themself!

JENNY: Don't be ridiculous. That's no reason why I can't be like Chester.

POPO: But Chester—he makes plenty money.

JENNY: Yeah. Right. Now. But he has to leave home to do it, see? I want a career, too. So what if I never get married?

AMA: Jenny! You must remember—you come from family of See-goh-poh. She was a great evangelist.

JENNY: I know about See-goh-poh. She was your aunt.

AMA: First in family to become Christian.

POPO: She make this family chosen by God.

JENNY: To do what? Clean teeth?

AMA: Jenny!

JENNY: Look, See-goh-poh never got married because of her work, right?

AMA: See-goh-poh was marry to God.

POPO: When Di-gou arrive, he will tell you his testimony. How See-goh-poh change his life.

AMA: Before, he is like you. *(To Popo)* You remember?

POPO: Yes. He is always so fussy.

JENNY: I'm not fussy.

AMA: Stubborn.

POPO: Complain this, complain that.

JENNY: I'm not complaining!

AMA: He will be very happy to meet you. Someone to complain with.

JENNY: I'm just telling you, there's no such thing as a dancing dental technician!

AMA: Good. You will be new discovery.

POPO: When Di-gou is a little boy, he never play with other children. He only read the books. Read books—and play tricks.

AMA: He is very naughty.

POPO: He tell other children there are ghosts hide inside the tree, behind the bush, in the bathroom at night.

AMA: One day, he feed snail poison to gardener.

POPO: Then, when he turns eight year old, See-goh-poh decide she will bring him on her evangelism tour. When he return, he had the tongue of fire.

JENNY: Oh, c'mon—those kind of things only happened in China.

AMA: No—they can happen here as well.

POPO: Di-gou at eight, he goes with See-goh-poh on her first evangelism tour—they travel all around Fukien—thirty day and night, preach to all villages. Five hundred people accept Christ on these thirty day, and See-goh-poh heal many sick, restore ear to deaf, put tongue in mouth of dumb, all these thing and cast out the demon. Perhaps even one dead man—dead and wither—he rise up from his sleep. Di-gou see all this while carry See-goh-poh's bag and bring her food, ah? After thirty day, they return home. We have large banquet—perhaps twelve different dish that night—outside—underneath—ah—cloth. After we eat, See-goh-poh say, "Now is time for Family Devotions, and this time, he will lead." See-goh-poh point to Di-gou, who is still a boy, but he walk up in front of table and begin to talk and flame begin to come from his mouth, over his head. Fire. Fire, all around. His voice—so loud—praise and testify the miracle of God. Louder and louder, more and more fire, 'til entire sky fill with light, does not seem to be night, like middle of day, like twelve noon. When he finish talk, sun has already rise, and cloth over our head, it is all burn, gone, ashes blow away.

(Joanne enters, pulling Chester behind. He carries a suitcase.)

JOANNE: Look who's here!

POPO: Chester—good you decide to come.

JOANNE: He looked lost. This house isn't that big, you know. *(Exits)*

AMA *(To Chester)*: You come for reunion with Di-gou. Very good.

CHESTER: Uh—look, I really can't stay. I have to finish packing.

AMA: You must stay—see Di-gou!

CHESTER: But I'm leaving tomorrow.

(Doorbell.)

Oh, no.

JOANNE *(Simultaneously)*: Can someone get that?

JENNY *(Simultaneously)*: Too late!

POPO: Di-gou!

AMA *(To Chester)*: You must! This will be Di-gou!

(Wilbur crosses with basket, now full of chicken bones.)

WILBUR: I'll get it. Chester, good to see you made it. *(Exits)*

JENNY: He almost didn't.

CHESTER: I'm really short on time. I gotta go. I'll see you tomorrow at the airport.

POPO: Chester! When Di-gou arrive, he must see whole family! You stay!

(Chester pauses, decides to stay.)

CHESTER *(To Jenny)*: This is ridiculous. I can't stay.

JENNY: I always have to. Just grin a lot when you meet this guy. Then everyone will be happy.

CHESTER: I don't wanna meet this guy!

(Wilbur enters with Hannah and Robert, who are Chester's parents. Hannah is Popo's daughter. She is five years older than Joanne.)

WILBUR *(To Robert)*: What? What do you mean?

(Ama stands on a chair and begins to make a speech:)

AMA: Di-gou, thirty year have pass since we last see you—

WILBUR *(To Ama)*: Not now, Ma.

AMA: Do you still love God?

ROBERT *(To Wilbur)*: What do you mean, "What do you mean?" That's what I mean.

HANNAH: He wasn't there, Wilbur. *(To Ama)* Auntie! Di-gou isn't with us.

AMA: What? How can this be?

ROBERT: Those Chinese airliners—all junk stuffs—so inefficient.

AMA: Where is he?

POPO *(To Robert)*: You sure you look close?

ROBERT: What "look close"? We just waited for everyone to get off the plane.

AMA: Where is he?

HANNAH *(To Ama)*: We don't know, Auntie! *(To Chester)* Chester, are you packed?

AMA: Don't know?

CHESTER *(To Hannah)*: No, I'm not. And I'm really in a hurry.

HANNAH: You're leaving tomorrow! Why aren't you packed?
CHESTER: I'm trying to, Mom.

(Robert pulls out a newspaper clipping, shows it to Chester.)

ROBERT: Look, son, I called the Chinese paper, used a little of my influence—they did a story on you. Here—
CHESTER *(Looks at clipping)*: I can't read this, Dad! It's in Chinese!
ROBERT *(Takes back clipping)*: Little joke, there.
AMA *(To anyone who will listen)*: Where is he?
HANNAH *(To Ama)*: Auntie, ask Wilbur. *(To Chester)* Get packed!
CHESTER: All right!
WILBUR *(Trying to explain to Ama)*: Well, Mom, they said he wasn't at—
AMA *(Ignoring Wilbur totally)*: Where is he?!

(Robert continues to study the newspaper clipping, points a section out to Chester.)

ROBERT: Here—this is where it talks about my bank.
CHESTER: I'm going to pack.
HANNAH *(To Chester)*: Going?
CHESTER *(To Hannah)*: You said I should—
HANNAH *(To Chester)*: You have to stay and see Di-gou!

(Wilbur makes another attempt to explain the situation to Ama.)

WILBUR: See, Mom, I guess—
AMA *(Ignoring him again)*: Where is he?

(Robert continues studying his clipping, oblivious.)

ROBERT *(Translating, to Chester)*: It says, "Great Chinese violinist will conduct and solo with New York Philharmonic."
CHESTER: What? It says what?
HANNAH *(To Chester)*: You came without being packed?

(Ama decides to look for Di-gou on her own and starts searching the house.)

AMA: Di-gou! Di-gou!

WILBUR *(Following Ama)*: Ma, listen. I'll explain.

HANNAH *(To Chester)*: How can you be so inefficient?

CHESTER *(To Robert)*: Dad, I just got a job playing in the violin section in Boston.

AMA: Di-gou! Di-gou!

CHESTER *(To Robert)*: I'm not conducting, and—

ROBERT *(To Chester)*: Ssssh! I know. But good publicity— for the bank.

HANNAH *(To Chester)*: Well, I'll help you pack later. But you have to stay 'til Di-gou arrives. Sheesh!

CHESTER: I can't believe this!

AMA *(Continuing her search)*: Di-gou! Are you already in bathroom? *(Exits)*

HANNAH *(To Ama)*: Auntie, he wasn't at the airport! *(To Wilbur)* Why didn't you tell her?

WILBUR *(Following Ama)*: I'm trying! I'm trying! *(Exits)*

ROBERT: It's those Communist airlines, I'm telling you. Inefficient.

HANNAH: We asked at the desk. They didn't have a flight list.

AMA *(Entering)*: Then where is he?

WILBUR *(Entering, in despair)*: Joanne, will you come here?

ROBERT: They probably left him in Guam.

POPO *(To Robert)*: We give you that photograph. You remember to bring it?

ROBERT: Of course I remembered.

HANNAH *(To Popo)*: Mom, it's not Robert's fault.

POPO *(To Hannah, referring to Robert)*: Should leave him in car.

HANNAH: I tried.

ROBERT: In the car?

HANNAH: He wanted to come in.

ROBERT: It's hot in the car!

AMA *(To Robert)*: Suffer, good for you.

POPO *(To Hannah)*: You cannot control your husband.

ROBERT: I suffer enough.

HANNAH: He said he could help.

POPO: He is wrong again.

AMA: What to do now?

(Jenny exits in the confusion; Joanne enters.)

JOANNE: What's wrong now?

WILBUR: They lost your uncle.

JOANNE: Who lost him?

HANNAH: We didn't lose him.

AMA *(To Robert)*: You ask at airport desk?

ROBERT: I'm telling you, he's in Guam.

JOANNE *(To Hannah)*: How could you lose a whole uncle?

HANNAH: We never had him to begin with!

JOANNE: So where is he?

ROBERT: Guam, I'm telling—!

POPO *(To Robert)*: Guam, Guam! Shut mouth or go there yourself!

HANNAH *(A general announcement)*: We don't know where he is!

JOANNE: Should I call the police?

WILBUR: You might have looked longer at the airport.

HANNAH: That's what I said, but *(Referring to Robert)* he said, "Aaah, too much trouble!"

POPO *(To Robert)*: See? You do not care about people from other provinces besides Shanghai.

ROBERT *(To Popo)*: Mom, I care. It's just that—

POPO *(To Robert)*: Your father trade with Japanese during war.

WILBUR: Huh?

ROBERT: Mom, let's not start that.

POPO: Not like our family. We die first!

WILBUR: What's all this about?

ROBERT: Hey, let's not bring up all this other junk, right?

POPO *(To Robert)*: You are ashamed.

ROBERT: The airport is a big place.

WILBUR *(To Robert)*: Still, you should've been able to spot an old Chinese man.

ROBERT: Everyone on that plane was an old Chinese man!

AMA: True. All Communist look alike.

HANNAH: Hold it, everybody! *(Pause)* Listen, Di-gou has this address, right?

AMA: No.

HANNAH: No? *(To Popo)* Mom, you said he did.

POPO: Yes. He does.

AMA *(To Popo)*: Yes? But I did not write to him.

POPO: I did.

AMA: Now, Communist—they will know this address.

POPO: Never mind.

AMA: No safety. Bomb us.

HANNAH: Okay, he has this address, and he can speak English—after all, he went to medical school here, right? So he shouldn't have any problem.

JOANNE: What an introduction to America.

HANNAH: All we can do is wait.

ROBERT: We went up to all these old Chinese men at the air-port, asked them, "Are you our Di-gou?" They all said yes. What could we do? They all looked drunk, bums.

JOANNE: Maybe they're all still wandering through the metal detectors, looking for their families, and will continue 'til they die.

(Chester wanders onto the tennis court, observes the fol-lowing section from far upstage.)

I must have been only about seven the last time Di-gou visited us in the Philippines.

AMA: Less.

JOANNE: Maybe less.

WILBUR: Honey, I'm sure everyone here has a memory, too. You don't see them babbling about it, do you?

JOANNE: The last thing I remember about Di-gou, he was trying to convince you grown-ups to leave the Philippines and return to China. There was a terrible fight—one of the worst that ever took place in our complex. I guess he wanted you to join the Revolution. The fight was so loud that all our servants gathered around the windows to watch.

AMA: They did this?

POPO: Shoot them.

JOANNE: I guess this was just around 1949. Finally, Di-gou left, calling you all sorts of terrible names. On his way out, he set fire to one of our warehouses. All us kids sat around while the servants tried to put it out.

POPO: No. That was not a warehouse.

HANNAH: Yeah, Joanne—the warehouses were concrete, remember?

JOANNE *(To Hannah)*: But don't you remember a fire?

HANNAH: Yes.

POPO: I think he burn a pile of trash.

ROBERT *(To Wilbur)*: I know how you feel. They're always yap-yap-yapping about their family stories—you'd think they were the only family in China. *(To Hannah)* I have memories, too.

HANNAH: You don't remember anything. You have a terrible memory.

ROBERT: Look, when I was kidnapped, I didn't know—

HANNAH: Sssssh!

JOANNE: Quiet, Robert!

POPO: Like broken record, ghang, ghang, ghang.

WILBUR *(To Robert)*: I tell you what: you wanna take a look at my collection of tax shelters?

ROBERT: Same old stuff?

WILBUR: No. Some new ones.

(Robert and Wilbur exit. Di-gou appears on the tennis court; only Chester sees him, but Chester says nothing. Chester watches Di-gou watching the women.)

JOANNE: Anyway, he set fire to something and the flames burned long into the night. One servant was even killed in it, if I remember correctly. I think Matthew's nursemaid was trying to put it out when her dress caught fire and, like a fool, she ran screaming all over the complex. All the adults were too busy to hear her, I guess, and all the kids just sat there and watched this second fire, moving in circles and screaming. By morning, both fires were out, and our tutors came as usual. But that day, nothing functioned just right—I think the water pipes broke in Sah-Zip's room, the cars wouldn't start—something—all I remember is servants running around all day with one tool or another. And that was how Di-gou left Manila for the last time. Left Manila and returned to China—in two fires— one which moved—and a great rush of handymen.

(Di-gou has made his way to sitting in their midst in the sunroom. He puts down his suitcase. They all turn and see him. He sticks his thumb out, as if for hitchhiking, but his thumb is pointed down instead of up.)

DI-GOU: "Going my way?"

AMA: Di-gou!

DI-GOU: "Hey, baby, got a lift?"

POPO: You see? Our family members will always return.

JOANNE *(To Di-gou)*: Are you—? Oh, you're—? Well, nice—how did you get here?

DI-GOU *(Pulls a book out of his jacket)*: Our diplomacy handbook. Very useful.

POPO: Welcome to America!

DI-GOU *(Referring to the handbook)*: It says, "When transportation is needed, put your thumb as if to plug a hole."

(Ama stands on the chair again.)

AMA: Di-gou, thirty year have passed—

DI-GOU *(Still reading)*: "And say, 'Going my way?'"

AMA: Do you still believe in God?

DI-GOU: "Or, 'Hey, baby, got a lift?'"

AMA: Do you?

HANNAH *(To Ama)*: Auntic, he's explaining something.

DI-GOU: It worked! I am here!

AMA *(Getting down off chair)*: Still as stubborn as before.

DI-GOU: Hello, my sisters.

POPO: Hello, Di-gou. This is my daughter, Hannah.

HANNAH *(To Di-gou)*: Were you at the airport? We were waiting for you.

DI-GOU: Hannah. Oh, last time, you were just a baby.

AMA *(Introducing Joanne)*: And Joanne, remember?

JOANNE: Hello, Di-gou. How was your flight?

DI-GOU: Wonderful, wonderful.

POPO: Where is Chester? Chester!

(Chester enters the lanai.)

Him—this is number-one grandson.

DI-GOU: Oh, you are Chester. You are the violinist, yes?

CHESTER: You're Di-gou?

DI-GOU: Your parents are so proud of you.

HANNAH: We are not. He's just a kid who needs to pack.

AMA: Where is Jenny? Jenny!

HANNAH *(To Di-gou)*: We figured you'd be able to get here by yourself.

DI-GOU: Oh, yes.

(Di-gou sticks out his thumb. Jenny enters.)

JOANNE: Jenny! Say, "Hi, Di-gou."

JENNY: Hi, Di-gou.

DI-GOU *(To Joanne)*: This is your daughter?

JOANNE: Yes. Jenny. *(Pause)* Jenny, say, "Hi, Di-gou."

JENNY: Mom, I just did!

JOANNE: Oh. Right.

JENNY: Will you cool out?

DI-GOU: Jenny, the last time I saw your mother, she was younger than you are now.

JENNY: He's kinda cute.

JOANNE: Jenny, your granduncle is not cute.

DI-GOU: Thank you.

JENNY *(To Joanne)*: Can I go now?

AMA: Why you always want to go?

JENNY: Sorry, Ama. Busy.

JOANNE *(Allowing Jenny to leave)*: All right.

DI-GOU *(To Jenny)*: What are you doing?

JENNY: Huh? Reading.

DI-GOU: Oh. Schoolwork.

JENNY: Nah. *Vogue. (Exits)*

JOANNE: I've got to see about dinner. *(To Hannah)* Can you give me a hand? I want to use my new Cuisinart.

HANNAH: All right. What do you want to make?

JOANNE: I don't know. What does a Cuisinart do?

(Hannah and Joanne exit; Di-gou, Ama, Popo and Chester are left in the sunroom.)

AMA: Di-gou, thirty year have pass. Do you still love God?

DI-GOU: Thirty-three.

AMA: Ah?

POPO: 1949 to 1982. Thirty-three. He is correct.

AMA: Oh. But you do still love God? Like before?

DI-GOU: You know, sisters, after you left China, I learned that I never did believe in God.

(Pause.)

AMA: What!

POPO: How can you say this?

CHESTER: Ama, Popo, don't start in on that—he just got here.

POPO: You defend him?

AMA *(To Chester and Di-gou while chasing Chester out to tennis court)*: You both are influence by bad people.

POPO: Spend time with bums! Communist bum, musician bum, both same.

DI-GOU: Just to hear my sisters after all these years—you may speak whatever you like.

AMA: Do you still love God?

DI-GOU: I have much love.

AMA: For God?

DI-GOU: For my sisters.

(Pause.)

POPO: You are being very difficult.

AMA: You remember when you first become Christian?

POPO: You travel with See-goh-poh on her first evangelism tour? Before we move to Philipines and you stay in China? Remember? You speak tongues of fire.

DI-GOU: I was only eight years old. That evening is a blur to me.

AMA: Tonight—we have family devotions. You can speak again. Miracles. You still believe in miracles?

DI-GOU: It is a miracle that I am here again with you!

POPO: Why you always change subject? You remember Ah Hong? Your servant? How See-goh-poh cast out his opium demon?

DI-GOU: I don't think that happened.

AMA: Yes! Remember? After evangelism tour—she cast out his demon.

POPO: Ah Hong tell stories how he eats opium, then he can see everything so clear, like—uh—glass. He can see even through wall, he say, and can see—ah—all the way through floor. Yes! He say he can see through ground, all the way to hell. And he talk with Satan and demon who pretend to be Ah Hong's dead uncles. You should remember.

DI-GOU: I vaguely recall some such stories.

(Di-gou opens up his suitcase during Popo's following speech and takes out two small Chinese toys and a small Chinese flag. He shows them to Popo, but she tries to ignore them.)

POPO: Demon pretend to be ghost, then show himself everyplace to Ah Hong—in kitchen, in well, in barn, in street of village. Always just sit there, never talk, never move, just sit. So See-goh-poh come, call on God, say only, "Demon begone."

AMA: And from then on, no more ghost, no more opium.

POPO: You—you so happy, then. You say, you will also cast out the demon.

DI-GOU: We were all just children. *(He lines the toys up on the floor)*

AMA: But you have faith of a child.

DI-GOU: Ah Hong didn't stop eating opium, though. He just needed money. That's why two years later, he was fired.

AMA: Ah Hong never fired!

POPO: I do not think so.

DI-GOU: Yes, my tenth, eleventh birthday, he was fired.

AMA: No—remember? Ah Hong die many year later—just before you come to America for college.

DI-GOU: No, he was fired before then.

POPO: No. Before you leave, go to college, you must prepare your own suitcase. *(To Ama)* Bad memory.

AMA: Brainwash.

(Robert and Wilbur enter; Chester exits off the tennis court. Robert and Wilbur surround Di-gou.)

ROBERT AND WILBUR: Welcome!

WILBUR: How you doing, Di-gow?

ROBERT *(Correcting Wilbur)*: Di-gou!

WILBUR: Oh, right. "Di-gou."

ROBERT *(To Di-gou)*: We tried to find you at the airport.

WILBUR *(To Di-gou)*: That means "second brother."

ROBERT: So, you escaped the Communists, huh?

WILBUR: Robert and I were just—

ROBERT: Little joke, there.

WILBUR: —looking at my collection of tax shelters.

ROBERT: China's pretty different now, huh?

WILBUR: You care to take a look?

ROBERT: I guess there's never a dull moment—

WILBUR: Probably no tax shelters, either.

ROBERT: —waiting for the next cultural revolution.

WILBUR: Oh, Robert!

ROBERT: Little joke, there.

WILBUR *(To Di-gou, referring to Robert)*: That's how he does business.

ROBERT: Of course, I respect China.

WILBUR: He says these totally outrageous things.

ROBERT: But your airlines—so inefficient.

WILBUR: And people remember him.

ROBERT: How long were you in Guam?

WILBUR *(To Robert)*: He wasn't in Guam!

ROBERT: No?

WILBUR *(To Di-gou)*: Well, we're going to finish up the tour.

ROBERT: My shelters are all at my house.

WILBUR: Feel free to come along.

ROBERT *(Referring to Wilbur)*: His are kid stuff. Who wants land in Montana?

WILBUR *(To Robert)*: Hey—I told you. I need the loss.

(Wilbur and Robert exit, leaving Di-gou with Ama and Popo. There is a long silence.)

DI-GOU: Who are they?

POPO: Servants.

AMA: Don't worry. They will eat outside. In America, servants do not take over their masters' house.

DI-GOU: What are you talking about?

AMA: We know. In China now, servants beat their masters.

DI-GOU: Don't be ridiculous. I have a servant. A chauffeur.

(Robert reenters.)

ROBERT: Hey, Di-gou—we didn't even introduce ourselves.

DI-GOU: Oh, my sisters explained it to me.

ROBERT: I'm Robert. Hannah's my wife. *(He puts his arm around Di-gou)* When we married, I had nothing. I was working in grocery stores, fired from one job after another. But she could tell—I had a good heart.

DI-GOU: It is good to see servants marrying into the moneyed ranks. We are not aware of such progress by even the lowest classes.

(Pause.)

ROBERT: Huh?

DI-GOU: To come to this—from the absolute bottom of society.

ROBERT: Wait, wait. I mean, sure, I made progress, but "the bottom of society"? That's stretching it some, wouldn't you say?

DI-GOU: Did you meet Hannah while preparing her food?

ROBERT: Huh? No, we met at a foreign students' dance at UCLA.

DI-GOU: Oh. You attended university?

ROBERT: Look, I'm not a country kid. It's not like I was that poor. I'm from Shanghai, you know.

POPO *(To Robert)*: Ssssh! Neighbors will hear!

ROBERT: I'm cosmopolitan. So when I went to college, I just played around at first. That's the beauty of the free enterprise system, Di-gou. If you wanna be a bum, it lets you be a bum. I wasted my time, went out with all these American girls.

POPO: One girl.

ROBERT: Well, one was more serious, a longer commitment . . .

POPO: Minor.

DI-GOU: What?

POPO: He go out with one girl—only fifteen year old.

ROBERT: I didn't know!

POPO *(To Robert)*: How come you cannot ask?

ROBERT: I was just an FOB. This American girl—she talked to me—asked me out—kissed me on first date—and I thought, "Land of Opportunity!" Anyway, I decided to turn my back on China.

POPO *(To Di-gou)*: He cannot even ask girl how old.

ROBERT: This is my home. When I wanted to stop being a bum, make money, it let me. That's America!

DI-GOU: I also attended American university. Columbia Medical School.

ROBERT: Right. My wife told me.

POPO *(To Robert)*: But he does not date the minor!

ROBERT *(To Popo)*: How was I supposed to know? She looked fully developed!

(Ama and Popo exit in disgust, leaving Robert alone with Di-gou.)

(To Di-gou) Well, then, you must understand American ways.

DI-GOU: It has been some time since I was in America.

ROBERT: Well, it's improved a lot, lemme tell you. Look, I have a friend who's an immigration lawyer. If you want to stay here, he can arrange it.

DI-GOU: Oh, no. The thought never even—

ROBERT: I know, but listen. I did it. Never had any regrets. We might be able to get your family over, too.

DI-GOU: Robert, I cannot leave China.

ROBERT: Huh? Look, Di-gou, people risk their lives to come to America. If only you could talk to—to the boat people.

DI-GOU: Uh—the food here looks very nice.

ROBERT: Huh? Oh, help yourself. Go ahead.

DI-GOU: Thank you. I will wait.

ROBERT: No, go on!

DI-GOU: Thank you, but—

ROBERT: Look, in America, there's so much, we don't have to be polite at all!

DI-GOU: Please—I'm not yet hungry.

ROBERT: Us Chinese, we love to eat, right? Well, here in America, we can be pigs!

DI-GOU: I'm not hungry.

ROBERT: I don't see why you can't—? Look. *(He picks up a bao)* See? *(He stuffs the whole thing into his mouth)* Pigs!

DI-GOU: Do you mind? I told you, I'm not—

ROBERT: I know. You're not hungry. Think I'm hungry? No, sir! What do I have to do to convince you? Here. *(He drops a tray of guo-tieh on the ground, begins stomping them)* This is the land of plenty!

DI-GOU: Ai! Robert!

(Robert continues stomping the guo-tieh like roaches.)

ROBERT: There's one next to your foot! *(He stomps it)* Gotcha!
DI-GOU: Please! It is not right to step on food!
ROBERT: "Right"? Now, see, that's your problem in the
P.R.C. —lots of justice, but you don't produce.

(Wilbur enters, catching Robert in the act.)

WILBUR: Robert? What are you—? What's all this?
ROBERT *(Stops stomping)*: What's the big deal? You got a
cleaning woman, don't you?

(Jenny enters.)

JENNY: Time to eat yet? *(She sees the mess)* Blaagh.

(Hannah enters.)

HANNAH: What's all this?
JENNY: Never mind.

*(Jenny exits; Wilbur points to Robert, indicating to Hannah
that Robert is responsible for the mess. Ama and Popo
also enter at this moment and see Wilbur's indication.)*

DI-GOU: In China, the psychological problems of wealth are
a great concern.
POPO: Ai! Who can clean up after man like this!
WILBUR: Robert, I just don't think this is proper.
AMA: Wilbur—not clean himself.
ROBERT: Quiet! You all make a big deal out of nothing!
DI-GOU: I am a doctor. I understand.
POPO: But Robert—he also has the fungus feet.
ROBERT: Shut up, everybody! Will you all just shut up? I
was showing Di-gou American ways!

(Wilbur takes Di-gou's arm.)

WILBUR *(To Di-gou)*: Uh—come out here. I'll show you
some American ways.

David Henry Hwang

(Wilbur and Di-gou go out to the tennis court.)

ROBERT *(To Wilbur)*: What do you know about American ways? You were born here!
POPO *(To Ama)*: Exercise—good for him.
ROBERT: Only us immigrants really know American ways!
POPO *(To Ama, pinching her belly)*: Good for here.
HANNAH *(To Robert)*: Shut up, dear. You've done enough damage today.

(Wilbur gets Di-gou a tennis racket.)

AMA *(To Popo, referring to Di-gou)*: In China, he receives plenty exercise. Whenever Communists, they come torture him.
WILBUR *(On tennis court, to Di-gou)*: I'll set up the machine. *(He goes off)*
ROBERT *(Looking through the glass walls at the tennis court)*: What's so American about tennis?
HANNAH *(To Robert)*: Yes, dear.
ROBERT: You all ruined it!
HANNAH: You ruined the *guo-tieh*, dear.
ROBERT: What's a few *guo-tieh* in defense of America?
DI-GOU *(To Wilbur)*: I have not played tennis since my college days at Columbia.
ROBERT *(To Hannah, referring to Di-gou)*: He was being so cheap! Like this was a poor country!
HANNAH: He's lived in America before, dear.
ROBERT: That was years ago. When we couldn't even buy a house in a place like this.
HANNAH: We still can't.
ROBERT: What?
HANNAH: Let's face it. We still can't afford—
ROBERT: That's not what I mean, stupid! I mean, when we wouldn't be able to because we're Chinese! He doesn't know the new America. I was making a point and you all ruined it!
HANNAH: Yes, dear. Now let's go in and watch the Betamax.

ROBERT: No!
HANNAH: C'mon!

(Robert and Hannah exit.

    On the tennis court, Di-gou and Wilbur stand next to each other, facing offstage. A machine offstage begins to shoot tennis balls at them, each ball accompanied by a small explosive sound. A ball goes by; Di-gou tries to hit it, but it is too high for him. Two more balls go by, but they are also out of Di-gou's reach. A fourth ball is shot out; it hits Wilbur.)

WILBUR: Aaaah!

(Balls are being shot out much faster now, pummeling Wilbur and Di-gou. Ama and Popo continue to sit in the sunroom, staring away from the tennis court, peaceful and oblivious.)

DI-GOU: Aaah!
WILBUR: I don't——! This never happened——!
DI-GOU: Watch out!
WILBUR: I'll turn off the machine.
DI-GOU: Good luck! Persevere! Overcome! Oh! Watch——!

(A volley of balls drives Wilbur back. Ama and Popo hear the commotion, look over to the tennis court. The balls stop shooting out.)

POPO: Tennis.
AMA: A fancy machine.

(Ama and Popo return to looking downstage. The balls begin again.)

WILBUR: Oh, no!
AMA: Wilbur—he is such a bad loser.
POPO: Good exercise, huh? His age—good for here. *(She pinches her belly)*
DI-GOU: I will persevere! *(He tries to get to the machine, is driven back)*

WILBUR: No! Di-gow!

DI-GOU: I am overcome!

WILBUR: Joanne!

(He begins walking like a guerrilla toward the machine and finally makes it offstage. The balls stop, presumably because Wilbur reached the machine. Di-gou runs off the court.)

DI-GOU *(Breathless)*: Is it time yet . . . that we may cease to have . . . such enjoyment?

(Wilbur crosses back onto the tennis court and into the lanai.)

WILBUR *(To offstage)*: Joanne! This machine's too fast. I don't pay good money to be attacked by my possessions! *(Exits)*

(Ama and Popo get up, exit into the house, applauding Di-gou as they go, for his exercise.)

AMA AND POPO *(Clapping)*: Good, good, very good!

(Di-gou is left alone on the tennis court. He is hit by a lone tennis ball. Then Chester enters, carrying a violin case. He has thrown that last ball.)

CHESTER: Quite a workout, there.

DI-GOU: America is full of surprises—why do all these products function so poorly?

CHESTER: Looks like "Made in the U.S." is gonna become synonymous with defective workmanship. *(Pause)* You wanna see my violin?

DI-GOU: I would love to.

CHESTER: I thought you might. Here. *(He removes the violin from its case)* See? No "Made in U.S." label.

DI-GOU: It is beautiful.

CHESTER: Careful! The back has a lacquer which never dries—so don't touch it, or you'll leave your fingerprints in it forever.

DI-GOU: Imagine that. After I die, someone could be playing a violin with my fingerprint.

CHESTER: Funny, isn't it?

DI-GOU: You know, I used to play violin.

CHESTER: Really?

DI-GOU: Though I never had as fine an instrument as this.

CHESTER: Try it. Go ahead.

DI-GOU: No. Please. I get more pleasure looking at it than I would playing it. But I would get the most pleasure hearing you play.

CHESTER: No.

DI-GOU: Please?

CHESTER: All right. Later. How long did you play?

DI-GOU: Some years. During the Cultural Revolution, I put it down.

CHESTER: Must've been tough, huh? *(He directs Di-gou's attention to the back of his violin)* Look—the back's my favorite part.

DI-GOU: China is my home, my work. I had to stay there. *(He looks at the back of the violin)* Oh—the way the light reflects—look. And I can see myself in it.

CHESTER: Yeah. Nice, huh?

DI-GOU: So you will take this violin and make music around the world.

CHESTER: Around the world? Oh, you probably got a misleading press clipping. See, my dad . . .

DI-GOU: Very funny.

CHESTER *(Smiling)*: Yeah. See, I'm just playing in the Boston Symphony. I'm leaving tomorrow.

DI-GOU: I am fortunate, then, to come today, or perhaps I would never meet you.

CHESTER: You know, I wasn't even planning to come here.

DI-GOU: That would be terrible. You know, in China, my wife and I had no children—for the good of the state. *(He moves to where he left the Chinese toys earlier in the act. He picks them up and studies them)* All these years, I try to imagine—what does Hannah look like? What does her baby look like? Now, I finally visit and what do I find? A young man. A violinist. The baby has long since disappeared. And I learn I'll never know the answer to my question.

(Silence.)

CHESTER: Di-gou, why did you come here?

DI-GOU: My wife has died, I'm old. I've come for my sisters.

CHESTER: Well, I hope you're not disappointed to come here and see your sisters, your family, carry on like this.

DI-GOU: They are still my sisters.

CHESTER: I'm leaving here. Like you did.

DI-GOU: But, Chester, I've found that I cannot leave the family. Today—look!—I follow them across an ocean.

CHESTER: You know, they're gonna start bringing you to church.

DI-GOU: No. My sisters and their religion are two different things.

CHESTER: No, they're not. You've been away. You've forgotten. This family breathes for God. Ever since your aunt, See-goh-poh.

DI-GOU: See-goh-poh is not the first member of this family.

CHESTER: She's the first Christian.

DI-GOU: There are faces back further than you can see. Faces long before the white missionaries arrived in China. Here. *(He holds Chester's violin so that its back is facing Chester, and uses it like a mirror)* Look here. At your face. Study your face and you will see—the shape of your face is the shape of faces back many generations—across an ocean, in another soil. You must become one with your family before you can hope to live away from it.

CHESTER: Oh, sure, there're faces. But they don't matter here. See-goh-poh's face is the only one that has any meaning here.

DI-GOU: No. The stories written on your face are the ones you must believe.

CHESTER: Stories? I see stories, Di-gou. All around me. This house tells a story. The days of the week tell a story—Sunday is a service, Wednesday and Friday are fellowship, Thursday is visitation. Even the furniture tells stories. Look around. See-goh-poh is sitting in every chair. There's nothing for me here.

DI-GOU: I am here.

CHESTER: You? All right. Here. *(He turns the back of the violin toward Di-gou, again using it like a mirror)* You look. You wanna know what I see? I see the shape of your face changing. And with it, a mind, a will, as different as the face. If you stay with them, your old self will go, and in its place will come a new man, an old man, a man who'll pray.

DI-GOU: Chester, you are in America. If you deny those who share your blood, what do you have in this country?

AMA *(From offstage)*: All right? Ready?

CHESTER: Your face is changing, Di-gou. Before you know it, you'll be praying and speaking in tongues.

AMA *(Still offstage)*: One, two, three, four!

(The sounds of a choir singing the "Hallelujah Chorus." Then, the choir, consisting of Wilbur, Joanne, Robert, Hannah and Popo, enters. They are led by Ama, who stands on the base of a movable podium which is being pushed into the room by Robert and Wilbur. The choir heads for the center of the room, where the podium comes to rest, with Ama still on it, and the "Hallelujah Chorus" ends. Robert begins singing the tenor aria "Every Valley Shall Be Exalted" from Handel's Messiah.)

ROBERT: "Every valley, every valley . . ."

HANNAH: Quiet, Robert!

ROBERT: But I want my solo!

JOANNE *(To Robert)*: Ssssh! We already decided this.

ROBERT *(Continuing to sing)*: ". . . shall be exalted . . ."

JOANNE *(Yelling offstage)*: Jenny!

AMA *(To Robert)*: Time for Family Devotions! Set up room!

(Everyone, except Di-gou, begins to arrange the room like a congregation hall, with the pulpit up front.)

ROBERT: But it's a chance to hear my beautiful voice.

JENNY *(From offstage)*: Yeah! What?

POPO *(To Robert)*: Hear at home, hear in car. Now set up room.

JOANNE *(Yelling offstage)*: Jenny! Devotions!

JENNY *(From offstage)*: Aw, Mom.

JOANNE *(Yelling offstage)*: Devotions!

JENNY *(Entering)*: All right.

ROBERT *(To Hannah)*: You know what this is? This is the breakdown of family authority.

HANNAH *(To Robert)*: You have all the authority, dear. Now shut up.

(Jenny goes over to Chester.)

JENNY: Hey, you still here? I thought for sure you'd have split by now.

CHESTER: I will.

JENNY: You gotta take it easier. Do like me. I act all lotus blossom for them. I say, "Hi, uncle this and auntie that." It's easy.

ROBERT: Look—all this free time. *(Sings)* "Every valley . . ."

POPO: Shoot him!

(The room is set up.)

AMA: We begin! Family Devotions!

(Ama flips a switch. A neon cross lights up.)

JENNY *(To Chester)*: Looks like a disco.

(Everyone sits down except Di-gou. The rest of the family waits for him. He walks over and sits down. Ama bows down to pray. Everyone bows except Chester and Di-gou, but since all other eyes are closed, no one notices their noncompliance. Ama begins to pray.)

AMA: Dear Father, when we think of your great mercy to this family, we can only feel so grateful, privilege to be family chose for your work. You claim us to be yours, put your mark on our heart.

(Chester gets up, picks up his violin, gets Di-gou's attention.)

Your blessing begin many year ago in China.

(Chester begins playing; his music serves as underscoring to Ama's prayer.)

When See-goh-poh, she hear your word—from missionary. Your spirit, it touch her heart, she accept you, she speak in tongue of fire.

(Chester begins to move out of the room as he plays.)

You continue, bless See-goh-poh. She become agent of God, bring light to whole family, until we are convert, we become shining light for you all through Amoy.

(Chester stops playing, looks at Di-gou, waves good-bye and exits. Di-gou gets up, walks to where Chester was standing before he left and waves good-bye.)

Let us praise your victory over Satan. Praise your power over demon. Praise miracle over our own sinful will. Praise your victory over even our very hearts. Amen.

(Ama conducts the choir in the ending of the "Hallelujah Chorus." As they sing, she notices Di-gou's chair is empty. She turns and sees him waving. Ama and Di-gou look at each other as the "Hallelujah Chorus" continues.)

ACT II

A moment later. As the curtain rises, all are in the same positions they occupied at the end of Act I. Ama and Di-Gou are looking at each other. The choir ends the "Hallelujah Chorus." Di-gou walks back toward his chair and sits. Ama notices that Chester's seat is empty.

AMA: Where is Chester?

HANNAH: I heard his violin.

AMA: This is Family Devotions.

ROBERT: The kid's got a mind of his own.

HANNAH: He probably went home to pack, Auntie. He's really in a hurry.

JENNY: Can I go look?

AMA: Why everyone want to go?

JENNY: But he forgot his suitcase. *(She points to the green suitcase, which Chester has left behind)*

POPO *(To Jenny)*: Di-gou . . . he will want to hear you give testimony.

(Jenny sits back down.)

AMA: Now—Special Testimony. Let us tell of God's blessing! Who will have privilege? Special Testimony! Who will be first to praise?

(Silence.)

He is in our presence! Open His arms to us!

(Silence.)

He is not going to wait forever—you know this! He is very busy!

(Robert stands up, starts to head for podium. Popo notices that Robert has risen, points to him.)

POPO: No! Not him!

AMA *(To Robert)*: He is very bored with certain people who say same thing over and over again.

WILBUR: Why don't we sit down, Robert?

JENNY: C'mon, Uncle Robert.

HANNAH: Dear, forget it, all right?

ROBERT: But she needed someone to start. I just—

POPO *(To Robert)*: She did not include you.

WILBUR: Can't you see how bored they are with that, Robert?

ROBERT: Bored?

WILBUR: Everybody else has forgotten it.

ROBERT: Forgotten it? They can't.   •

JOANNE: We could if you'd stop talking about it.

ROBERT: But there's something new!

WILBUR: Of course. There always is.

ROBERT: There is!

JOANNE *(To Wilbur)*: Don't pay attention, dear. It just encourages him.

WILBUR *(To Joanne)*: Honey, are you trying to advise *me* on how to be diplomatic?

JOANNE: I'm only saying, if you let Hannah—

WILBUR: You're a real stitch, you know that? You really are.

JOANNE: Hannah's good at keeping him quiet.

ROBERT: Quiet?

WILBUR *(To Joanne)*: Look, who was voted "Mr. Congeniality" at the club last week—you or me?

ROBERT: Hannah, who are you telling to be quiet?

HANNAH: Quiet, Robert.

WILBUR *(To Joanne)*: Afraid to answer? Huh? Who? Who was "Mr. Congeniality"? Tell me—were you "Mr. Congeniality"?

JENNY *(To Wilbur)*: I don't think she stood a chance, Dad.

WILBUR *(To Jenny)*: Who asked you, huh?

JENNY: "Mr. Congeniality," I think.

WILBUR: Don't be disrespectful.

AMA: We must begin Special Testimony! Who is first?

POPO: I talk.

JOANNE: Good.

POPO: Talk from here. *(She stands)* Long time since we all come here like this. I remember long ago, family leave China—the boat storm, storm, storm, storm, all around, Hannah cry. I think, "Aaah, why we have to leave China, go to Philippines?" But I remember Jonah, when he did not obey God, only then seas become—ah—dangerous. And ever after, after Jonah eaten by whale, God provide for him. So if God has plan for us, we live; if not *(She looks at Di-gou)* we die. *(She sits)* Okay. That's all.

(Everyone applauds.)

AMA: Very good! Who is next?

ROBERT: I said, I'd be happy to—

HANNAH: How about Jenny?

JENNY: Me?

JOANNE: Sure, dear, c'mon.

JENNY: Oh . . . well . . .

POPO *(To Di-gou)*: You see—she is so young, but her faith is old.

JENNY: After I do this, can I go see what's happened to Chester?

POPO *(To Jenny)*: First, serve God.

ROBERT: Let her go.

POPO: Then, you may see about Chester.

JENNY: All right. *(She walks to the podium)*

POPO *(To Di-gou)*: I will tell you what each sentence meaning.

DI-GOU: I can understand quite well.

POPO: No. You are not Christian. You need someone—like announcer at baseball game—except announce for God.

JENNY *(At podium, she begins testimony)*: First, I want to say that I love you all very much. I really do.

POPO *(To Di-gou)*: That meaning is, she love God.

JENNY: And I appreciate what you've done for me.

POPO *(To Di-gou)*: She love us because we show her God.

JENNY: But I guess there are certain times when even love isn't enough.

POPO *(To Di-gou)*: She does not have enough love for you. You are not Christian.

JENNY: Sometimes, even love has its dark side.

POPO *(To Di-gou)*: That is you.

JENNY: And when you find that side, sometimes you have to leave in order to come back in a better way.

POPO *(To Di-gou)*: She cannot stand to be around you.

JENNY: Please. Remember what I said, and think about it later.

POPO *(To Di-gou)*: You hear? Think!

JENNY: Thank you.

(Everyone applauds.)

AMA: Good, good.

JENNY: Can I go now?

ROBERT *(To Hannah)*: What was she talking about?

AMA *(To Jenny)*: Soon, you can be best testifier—do testimony on TV.

JENNY: Can I go now?

JOANNE: All right, Jenny.

JENNY: Thanks. *(Exits)*

ROBERT *(To Popo)*: Why don't you interpret for *me*? I didn't understand what she was talking about. Not a bit.

POPO: Good.

ROBERT: Good? Don't you want me to be a better Christian?

POPO: No. Not too good. Do not want to live in same part of Heaven as you.

ROBERT: Why not? It'll be great, Popo. We can tell stories, sing—

POPO: In Heaven, hope you live in basement.

ROBERT: Basement? C'mon, Popo, I'm a celebrity. They wouldn't give me the basement. They'll probably recognize my diplomacy ability, make me ambassador.

JOANNE: To Hell?

ROBERT: Well, if that's the place they send ambassadors.

POPO: Good. You be ambassador.

AMA: Special Testimony! Who is next?

ROBERT *(Asking to be recognized)*: Ama?

AMA *(Ignoring him)*: *Who is next?*

ROBERT: Not me. I think Wilbur should speak.

AMA *(Disgusted)*: Wilbur?

WILBUR: Me?

ROBERT: Yeah.

WILBUR: Well, I don't really . . .

ROBERT: Tell them, Wilbur. Tell them what kind of big stuffs happen to you. Tell them how important you are.

WILBUR: Well, I . . .

AMA *(Reluctantly)*: Would you . . . like to speak . . . Wilbur?

WILBUR: Well, I'd be honored, but if anyone else would rather . . .

ROBERT: We want to hear what you have to be proud of.

WILBUR: All right.

(Wilbur takes the podium; Ama scurries away.)

Uh—well, it's certainly nice to see this family reunion. Uh—last week, I was voted Mr. Congeniality at the club.

ROBERT: What papers was it in?

WILBUR: Huh?

ROBERT: Was it in the *L.A. Times*? Front page? Otis Chandler's paper?

HANNAH *(A rebuff)*: Robert!

POPO *(To Robert)*: Devotions is not question-and-answer for anyone except God.

ROBERT: God sometimes speaks through people, doesn't He?

POPO: He has good taste. Would not speak through you.

ROBERT *(Undaunted, to Wilbur)*: Show me one newspaper clipping. Just one!

WILBUR: Well, besides the *Valley Green Sheet* . . .

ROBERT: The *Valley Green Sheet?* Who pays for that? Junk. People line their birdcages with it.

WILBUR: Well, I suppose from a media standpoint, it's not that big a deal.

AMA *(To Joanne)*: What means "congeniality"?

JOANNE: It means "friendly," sort of.

ROBERT *(To Wilbur)*: So why are you talking about it? Waste our time?

WILBUR: Look, Robert, it's obviously a token of their esteem.

ROBERT: Junk stuffs. Little thing. Who cares?

AMA *(To herself)*: "Mr. Friendly"?

ROBERT: It's embarrassing. What if clients say to me, "You're a bank president but your relative can only get into the *Valley Green Sheet*"? Makes me lose face. They think my relatives are bums.

AMA *(To Joanne)*: He is "Mr. Friendly"?

WILBUR: Look, Robert, the business is doing real well. It's not like that's my greatest accomplishment.

AMA *(To Joanne)*: How can he be "Mr. Friendly"? He always kill and laugh.

JOANNE: Mom!

ROBERT *(To Wilbur)*: Does your business get in the paper?

WILBUR: Computer software happens to be one of the nation's fastest-growing—

ROBERT: So what? Lucky guess. Big deal.

WILBUR: It was an educated choice, not luck!

(Robert gets up, starts to head for the podium.)

ROBERT: Anyone can make money in America. What's hard is to become . . . a celebrity.

WILBUR: You're not a celebrity.

ROBERT: Yes, I am. That's the new thing. See, I just wanted to say that—

(Robert nudges Wilbur off the podium, takes his place.)

—when I was kidnapped, I didn't know if I would live or die.

POPO *(Turns and sees Robert at the podium)*: Huh?

JOANNE: Robert, forget it!

POPO: How did he get up there?

WILBUR *(To Joanne)*: I'm perfectly capable of handling this myself.

POPO: He sneak up there while we are bored!

WILBUR *(To Popo)*: I'm sorry you found my testimony boring.

ROBERT *(To Wilbur)*: It was. *(To the assemblage)* Now hear mine.

JOANNE: We've all heard it before.

HANNAH *(To Robert)*: They're tired, dear. Get down.

ROBERT: Why? They listened to Wilbur's stuff. Boring. Junk.

JOANNE: "I didn't know if I would live or die." "I didn't know if I would live or die."

ROBERT: Di-gou, he hasn't heard. Have you, Di-gou?

DI-GOU: Is this when you didn't know if you would live or die?

ROBERT: How did—? Who told him?

POPO: I cannot think of enough ways to shoot him! Rifle! Arrows!

HANNAH *(To Robert)*: Sit down!

ROBERT: But there's something new!

HANNAH: I think we better let him speak, or he'll never shut up.

ROBERT: She's right. I won't.

JOANNE: All right. Make it quick, Robert.

ROBERT: All right. As I was saying, I didn't know if I would live or die.

JOANNE: You lived.

ROBERT: But the resulting publicity has made me a celebrity. Everyplace I go, people come up to me—"Aren't you the one that got kidnapped?" When I tell them how much the ransom was, they can hardly believe it. They ask for my autograph. Now—here's the new thing. I met these clients last week, told them my story. Now, these guys are big shots and they say it would make a great movie. Yeah. No kidding. They made movies before. Not just regular movie, that's junk stuffs. We want to go where the big money is—we want to make a miniseries for TV. Like *Shogun*. I told them, they should take the story, spice it up a little, you know? Add some sex scenes—we were thinking that I could have some hanky-panky with one of my kidnappers—woman, of course—just for audience sake—like Patty Hearst. I told them I should be played by Marlon Brando. And I have the greatest title: *Not a Chinaman's Chance*. Isn't that a great title? *Not a Chinaman's Chance*. Beautiful. I can see the beginning already: I'm walking out of my office. I stop to help a man fixing a flat tire.

HANNAH: All right, dear. That's enough.

ROBERT: Meanwhile, my secretary is having sex with my kidnapper.

HANNAH: Kidnap! Kidnap! That's all I ever hear about!

ROBERT: But, Hannah, I didn't know if I would live or die.

HANNAH: I wish you'd never even been kidnapped.

JOANNE: Well, what about Wilbur?

WILBUR: Leave me out of this.

JOANNE: Wilbur, you could be kidnapped.

WILBUR: I know, I know. It just hasn't happened yet, that's all.

HANNAH: Listen, Joanne. Count your blessings. It's not that great a thing. If they live, they never stop talking about it.

ROBERT: But the publicity!—I sign newspapers all the time!

JOANNE: I'm just saying that Robert's not the only one worth kidnapping.

HANNAH: Joanne, no one's saying that.

AMA: Yes. We all desire Wilbur to be kidnapped also.

POPO: And Robert. Again. This time, longer.

JOANNE: I mean, Wilbur has a lot of assets.

ROBERT: Wilbur, maybe next time you can get kidnapped.

WILBUR: Never mind, honey.

JOANNE: You do.

WILBUR: I can defend myself.

ROBERT: But it takes more than assets to be kidnapped. You have to be cosmopolitan.

HANNAH: Hey, wait. What kind of example are we setting for Di-gou?

ROBERT: See? That's why I'm talking about it. To show Di-gou the greatness of America. I'm just an immigrant, Di-gou, an FOB—but in America, I get kidnapped.

HANNAH: I mean, a Christian example.

DI-GOU: Oh, do not worry about me. This is all very fascinating.

JOANNE *(To Robert)*: So, you think you're cosmopolitan, huh?

ROBERT: I am. Before they let me loose, those kidnappers— they respected me.

JOANNE: They probably let you go because they couldn't stand to have you in their car.

POPO: Probably you sing to them.

ROBERT: No. They said, "We've been kidnapping a long time, but—"

JOANNE: Because we can't stand to have you in our house!

(Pause.)

ROBERT *(To Joanne)*: Now what kind of example are you setting for Di-gou?

WILBUR: Joanne, just shut up, okay?

HANNAH *(To Di-gou)*: It's not always like this.

JOANNE *(To Wilbur)*: You never let me talk! You even let *(Referring to Robert)* him talk, but you never let me talk!

AMA *(To Joanne, referring to Wilbur)*: He cannot deprive you of right to speak. Look. No gun.

ROBERT: Joanne, I have to tell this because Di-gou is here.

DI-GOU: Me?

JOANNE *(To Robert)*: You tell it to waiters!

ROBERT: Joanne, I want *(Referring to Di-gou)* him to understand America. The American Dream. From rags to kidnap victim.

JOANNE *(To Robert)*: Well, I don't like you making Di-gou think that Wilbur's a bum.

WILBUR *(To Joanne)*: Dear, he doesn't think that.

JOANNE *(To Di-gou)*: You see, don't you, Di-gou? This house. Wilbur bought this.

DI-GOU: It is a palace.

JOANNE: It's larger than Robert's.

HANNAH: Joanne, how can you sink to my husband's level?

ROBERT: My house would be larger, but we had to pay the ransom.

POPO: Waste of money.

JOANNE: Look, all of you always put down Wilbur. Well, look at what he's done.

WILBUR *(To Joanne)*: Just shut up, all right?

JOANNE *(To Wilbur)*: Well, if you're not going to say it.

WILBUR: I don't need you to be my PR firm.

ROBERT *(To anybody)*: He doesn't have a PR firm. We do. Tops firm.

JOANNE *(To Wilbur)*: Let me say my mind!

WILBUR: There's nothing in your mind worth saying.

JOANNE: What?

WILBUR: Face it, honey, you're boring.

AMA *(To Wilbur)*: At least she does not torture!

WILBUR: Please! No more talking about torture, all right?

AMA: All right. I will be quiet. No need to torture me.

POPO *(To Di-gou)*: This small family disagreement.

JOANNE: So I'm boring, huh?

WILBUR *(To Joanne)*: Look, let's not do this here.

POPO *(To Di-gou)*: But power of God will overcome this.

JOANNE: I'm boring—that's what you're saying?

HANNAH: Joanne! Not in front of Di-gou!

JOANNE *(To Di-gou)*: All right. You're objective. Who do you think is more boring?

DI-GOU: Well, I can hardly—

WILBUR: Please, Joanne.

POPO *(To Di-gou)*: Do you understand how power of God will overcome this?

JOANNE *(Referring to Wilbur)*: He spends all his time with machines, and he calls me boring!

AMA: Di-gou, see the trials of this world?
WILBUR *(To Joanne)*: Honey, I'm sorry, all right?
JOANNE: Sure, you're sorry.
AMA *(To Di-gou)*: Argument, fight, no-good husbands.
WILBUR: "No-good husbands"?

(Robert, in disgust, exits into the house.)

AMA *(To Di-gou)*: Turn your eyes from this.

(Popo and Ama turn Di-gou's eyes from the fight.)

JOANNE *(To Wilbur, referring to Ama)*: She's right, you know.
WILBUR: All right, honey, let's discuss this later.
JOANNE: Later! Oh, right.

(Wilbur runs off into the house; Joanne yells after him.)

When we're with *your* family, that's when you want to
talk about my denting the Ferrari.
HANNAH: Joanne! Don't be so boring!
JOANNE *(To Hannah)*: With *our* family, it's "later."
AMA *(To Di-gou)*: Look up to God!

(Popo and Ama force Di-gou to look up.)

DI-GOU: Please!

*(Di-gou breaks away from the sisters' grip, but they
knock him down.)*

POPO: Now—is time to join family in Heaven.
AMA: Time for you to return to God.
HANNAH *(To Joanne)*: Look—they're converting Di-gou.
POPO: Return. Join us for eternity.
AMA: Pray now.

(Popo and Ama try to guide Di-gou to the neon cross.)

DI-GOU: Where are we going?
AMA: He will wash you in blood of the lamb.
POPO: Like when you are a child. Now! You bow down!
HANNAH: Ask God for His forgiveness.

JOANNE: You won't regret it, Di-gou.

DI-GOU: Do you mind? *(He breaks away)*

POPO: Why will you not accept Him?

AMA: There is no good reason.

DI-GOU: I want to take responsibility for my own life.

POPO: You cannot!

AMA: Satan is rule your life now.

DI-GOU: I am serving the people.

AMA: You are not.

POPO: You serve them, they all die, go to Hell. So what?

DI-GOU: How can you abandon China for this Western religion?

AMA: It is not.

DI-GOU: There is no God!

(Pause.)

AMA: There is too much Communist demon in him. We must cast out demon.

POPO: Now, tie him on table.

DI-GOU: This is ridiculous. Stop this.

(Ama and Popo grab Di-gou, tie him on the table.)

POPO: We have too much love to allow demon to live.

DI-GOU: What?

POPO *(To Joanne and Hannah, who are hesitating)*: Now!

DI-GOU: You can't—!

POPO: Now! Or demon will escape!

AMA: We must kill demon.

POPO: Shoot him!

AMA: Kill for good.

POPO: Make demon into *jok*!

DI-GOU: This is barbaric! You live with the barbarians, you become one yourself!

POPO: Di-gou, if we do not punish your body, demon will never leave.

AMA: Then you will return to China.

POPO: And you will die.

AMA: Go to Hell.

POPO: And it will be too late.

DI-GOU: I never expected Chinese children to tie down their elders.

(Di-gou is now securely tied to the table.)

HANNAH: All right. We're ready.

POPO: Now—give your testimony.

DI-GOU: I'll just lie here and listen, thank you.

AMA: You tell of God's mercies to you.

JOANNE: How He let you out of China.

AMA: Where you are torture.

JOANNE: Whipped.

POPO: After thirty year, He let you out. Praise Him!

DI-GOU: I will never do such a thing!

HANNAH: If you wait too long, He'll lose patience.

POPO: Now—tell of your trip with See-goh-poh.

AMA: The trip which began your faith.

DI-GOU: I was only eight years old. I don't remember.

POPO: Tell how many were convert on her tour.

HANNAH: Tell them, Di-gou.

DI-GOU: I cannot.

JOANNE: Why? Just tell the truth.

POPO: Tell how you saw the miracle of a great evangelist, great servant of God.

HANNAH: Tell them before they lose their patience.

DI-GOU: I'm sorry. I will not speak.

POPO: Then we are sorry, Di-gou, but we must punish your body. Punish to drive out the demon and make you speak.

HANNAH: Don't make them do this, Di-gou.

AMA: If you will not speak See-goh-poh's stories in language you know, we will punish you until you speak in tongue of fire.

(Ama hits Di-gou with an electrical cord, using it like a whip.)

JOANNE: Please, Di-gou!

David Henry Hwang

HANNAH: Tell them!

AMA: Our Lord was beat, nails drive through His body, for our sin. Your body must suffer until you speak the truth.

(Ama hits Di-gou.)

HANNAH: Tell them, See-goh-poh was a great evangelist.

AMA: You were on her evangelism tour—we were not— you must remember her converts, her miracle.

(Hit.)

JOANNE: Just tell them and they'll let you go!

AMA: Think of See-goh-poh! She is sit!

(Hit.)

Sit beside God. He is praising her! Praise her for her work in China.

(Chester enters the tennis court; he looks into the sunroom and sees Ama hit Di-gou.)

She is watching you!

(Hit. Chester tries to get into the sunroom, but the glass door is locked. He bangs on it, but everyone inside is shocked at Ama's ritual, and no one notices him. He exits off the tennis court, running.)

Praying for you! Want you to tell her story!

(Hit.)

We will keep you in float. Float for one second between life and death. Float until you lose will to hold to either—hold to anything at all.

(Ama quickly slips the electrical cord around Di-gou's neck, begins pulling on it. Joanne and Hannah run to get Ama off Di-gou. Chester enters from the house with Jenny close behind him. He pulls Ama off of Di-gou.)

CHESTER: Ama! Stop it!

(Di-gou suddenly breaks out of his bonds and rises up on the table. He grabs Chester. The barbecue bursts into flames. Di-gou, holding onto Chester, begins speaking in tongues.)

AMA *(Looking up from the ground)*: He is speaking in tongues! He has returned!

(Everyone falls to their knees. As Di-gou's babbling continues, Chester is suddenly filled with words, and begins interpreting Di-gou's words.)

CHESTER: Di-gou at eight goes with See-goh-poh on her first evangelism tour. Di-gou and See-goh-poh traveling through the summer heat to a small village in Fukien. Sleeping in the straw next to See-goh-poh. Hearing a sound. A human sound. A cry in my sleep. Looking up and seeing a fire. A fire and See-goh-poh. See-goh-poh is naked. Naked and screaming. Screaming with legs spread so far apart. So far that a mouth opens up. A mouth between her legs. A mouth that is throwing up blood, spitting out blood. More and more blood. See-goh-poh's hands making a baby out of the blood. See-goh-poh hits the blood baby. Hits the baby and the baby cries. Watching the baby at See-goh-poh's breast. Hearing the sucking.

(Ama and Popo spring up.)

POPO: Such a thing never happened!
AMA: See-goh-poh never did this!
POPO: This is not tongues. This is not God. This is demon!
CHESTER: Sucking. Praying. Sucking. Squeezing. Crying.
AMA: He is possess by demon!
CHESTER: Biting. Blood. Milk.
POPO: Both have the demon!
CHESTER: Blood and milk. Blood and milk running down.
AMA *(To the other women)*: You pray.
CHESTER: Running down, further and further down.

POPO: We must cast out the demon!

(Di-gou's words slowly become English, first overlapping, then overtaking Chester's translation. Chester becomes silent and exhausted, drops to the ground.)

CHESTER AND DI-GOU: Down. Down and into the fire. The fire down there. The fire down there.

(Di-gou breaks the last of his bonds, gets off the table.)

DI-GOU *(To the sisters)*: Your stories are dead now that you know the truth.

AMA: We have faith. We know our true family stories.

DI-GOU: You do not know your past.

AMA: Are you willing to match your stories against ours?

(Di-gou indicates his willingness to face Ama, and the two begin a ritualistic battle. Popo encourages Ama by speaking in tongues. Ama and Di-gou square off in seated positions, facing one another.)

We will begin. How many rooms in our house in Amoy?

DI-GOU: Eighteen. How many bedrooms?

AMA: Ten. What year was it built?

DI-GOU: 1893. What year was the nineteenth room added?

AMA: 1923.

DI-GOU: On whose instructions?

AMA: See-goh-poh.

DI-GOU: What year did See-goh-poh die?

AMA: 1945. What disease?

DI-GOU: Malaria. How many teeth was she missing?

AMA: Three.

DI-GOU: What villages were on See-goh-poh's evangelism tour?

(Silence.)

Do you know?

AMA: She preached to all villages in Fukien.

DI-GOU: Name one.

(Silence.)

Do you know? Your stories don't know. It never happened.
AMA: It did! What year was she baptized?

(Silence.)

What year was she baptized?
DI-GOU: She was never baptized.
AMA: You see? You don't remember.
DI-GOU: Never baptized.
AMA: It was 1921. Your stories do not remember.
DI-GOU: Who was converted on her evangelism tour?
AMA: Perhaps five hundred or more.
DI-GOU: Who? Name one.

(Silence.)

AMA: It is not important.
DI-GOU: You see? It never happened.
AMA: It did.
DI-GOU: You do not remember. You do not know the past.
See-goh-poh never preached.
AMA: How can you say this?
DI-GOU: She traveled.
AMA: To preach.
DI-GOU: To travel.
AMA: She visited many—
DI-GOU: I was there! She was thrown out—thrown out on
her evangelism tour when she tried to preach.

(Silence.)

AMA: It does not matter.
DI-GOU: You forced her to invent the stories.
AMA: We demand nothing!
DI-GOU: You expected! Expected her to convert all Amoy!
AMA: She did!
DI-GOU: Expected many miracles.
AMA: She did! She was a great—

DI-GOU: Expected her not to have a baby.

AMA: She had no husband. She had no baby. This is demon talk. Demon talk and lie.

DI-GOU: She turned away from God.

AMA: We will never believe this!

DI-GOU: On her tours she could both please you and see China.

(Popo's voice becomes weaker; she starts to falter.)

AMA: See-goh-poh was a great—

DI-GOU: Only on her tours could she see both China and her baby.

AMA: She was a great . . . a great evangelist . . . many . . .

DI-GOU: Where is she buried?

AMA: . . . many miracles . . .

DI-GOU: She is not buried within the walls of the church in Amoy.

AMA: . . . many miracle, a great evangelist . . .

(Popo collapses.)

DI-GOU: In her last moment, See-goh-poh wanted to be buried in Chinese soil, not Christian soil. You don't know. You were in the Philippines. *(Pause)* I come to bring you back to China. Come, sisters. To the soil you've forsaken with ways born of memories, of stories that never happened. Come, sisters. The stories written on your face are the ones you must believe.

(Ama rises from her chair.)

AMA: We will never believe this!

(Ama collapses back into her chair, closes her eyes. Silence.)

DI-GOU: Sisters?

(Silence.)

Sisters!

(Jenny, Chester, Joanne, Hannah and Di-gou stare at the two inert forms.)

CHESTER: Jenny! Jenny!

(Jenny goes to Chester's side.)

JOANNE: Hannah? Hannah—come here.

(Hannah does not move.)

HANNAH: I see.
JOANNE: No! Come here!
HANNAH: I know, Joanne. I see.
DI-GOU: Once again. Once again my pleas are useless. But now—this is the last time. I have given all I own.

(Popo and Ama have died. Di-gou picks up his suitcase and the Chinese toys, heads for the door.)

JOANNE *(To Di-gou)*: Are you leaving?
DI-GOU: Now that my sisters have gone, I learn. No one leaves America. And I desire only to drive an American car—very fast—down an American freeway. *(He exits)*
JOANNE *(Yelling after him)*: This is our home, not yours! Why didn't you stay in China! This is not your family!

(Jenny starts to break away from Chester, but he hangs onto her. Joanne turns, sees the figures of Ama and Popo.)

Wilbur! Wilbur, come here!
JENNY *(To Chester)*: Let go of me! Get away! *(She breaks away from Chester)* I don't understand this, but whatever it is, it's ugly and awful and causes people to die. It causes people to die and I don't want to have anything to do with it.

(Jenny runs out onto the tennis court and away. On her way, she passes Robert, who has entered onto the court. Robert walks into the sunroom. Silence.)

ROBERT: What's wrong with her? She acts like someone just died.

(Silence. Robert pulls up a chair next to Chester.)

Let's chitchat, okay?
CHESTER: Sure, Dad.
ROBERT: So, how's Dorrie?

(Silence.)

How much they paying you in Boston?

(Silence.)

Got any newspaper clippings?

(Silence. Chester gets up, picks up his suitcase, walks onto the tennis court and shuts the glass doors. Joanne and Hannah stare at Ama and Popo. Robert sits, staring off into space.

Chester stands where Di-gou stood at the beginning of the play. He turns around and looks through the glass door onto the scene.

The lights begin to dim until there is one single spotlight on Chester's face. The shape of Chester's face begins to change.)

END OF PLAY

THE SOUND

OF A VOICE

(1983)

Production History

The Sound of a Voice opened with *The House of Sleeping Beauties* under the title *Sound and Beauty* at The Joseph Papp Public Theater/New York Shakespeare Festival (Joseph Papp, Producer), in New York City on November 6, 1983. It was directed by John Lone and assisted by Lenore Kletter; the set design was by Andrew Jackness; the costume design was by Lydia Tanji; the lighting design was by John Gisondi; and the music was by Lucia Hwong. There were two dancers, Elizabeth Fong Sung and Ching Valdes, in this production. The cast was as follows:

WOMAN	Natsuko Ohama
MAN	John Lone

Characters

WOMAN (Hanako), Japanese, forties or fifties.
MAN, Japanese, fifties.

Place

Woman's house, in a remote corner of a forest.

Time

Scene One: evening.
Scene Two: dawn.
Scene Three: day.
Scene Four: night.
Scene Five: day.
Scene Six: night.
Scene Seven: morning.
Scene Eight: day.
Scene Nine: night.

Definition

shakuhatchi: Japanese end-blown bamboo flute.

Scene One

*It is evening. Woman warms tea for man. Man rubs himself,
trying to get warm. The room they are in is sparsely fur-
nished, except for one shelf on which stands a vase of brightly
colored flowers. The flowers stand out in sharp contrast to the
starkness of the room.*

MAN: You are very kind to take me in.
WOMAN: This is a remote corner of the world. Guests are
    rare.
MAN: The tea—you pour it well.
WOMAN: No.
MAN: The sound it makes—in the cup—very soothing.
WOMAN: That is the tea's skill, not mine. *(She hands the cup
    to him)* May I get you something else? Rice, perhaps?
MAN: No.
WOMAN: Some vegetables?
MAN: No, thank you.
WOMAN: Fish? *(Pause)* It is at least two days walk to the
    nearest village. I saw no horse. You must be very hungry.
    You would do a great honor to dine with me. Guests
    are rare.
MAN: Thank you.

*(Woman gets up, leaves. Man gets up, walks to kitchen
door, listens. He crosses to the vase of flowers. He touches
them. Quickly, he takes one of the flowers from the vase,
hides it in his clothes. Woman reenters. She carries a tray
with food.)*

WOMAN: Please. Eat. It will give me great pleasure.

MAN: This—this is magnificent.

WOMAN: Eat.

MAN: Thank you. *(He motions for Woman to join him)*

WOMAN: No, thank you.

MAN: This is wonderful. The best I've tasted.

WOMAN: You are reckless in your flattery, sir. But anything you say, I will enjoy hearing. It's not even the words. It's the sound of a voice, the way it moves through the air.

MAN: How long has it been since you last had a visitor?

(Pause.)

WOMAN: I don't know.

MAN: Oh?

WOMAN: I lose track. Perhaps five months ago, perhaps ten years, perhaps yesterday. I don't consider time when there is no voice in the air. It's pointless. Time begins with the entrance of a visitor, and ends with his exit.

MAN: And in between? You don't keep track of the days? You can't help but notice—

WOMAN: Of course I notice.

MAN: Oh.

WOMAN: I notice, but I don't keep track. *(Pause)* May I bring out more?

MAN: More? No. No. This was wonderful.

WOMAN: I have more.

MAN: Really—the best I've had.

WOMAN: You must be tired. Did you sleep in the forest last night?

MAN: Yes.

WOMAN: Or did you not sleep at all?

MAN: I slept.

WOMAN: Where?

MAN: By a waterfall. The sound of the water put me to sleep. It rumbled like the sounds of a city. You see, I can't sleep in too much silence. It scares me. It makes me feel that I have no control over what is about to happen.

WOMAN: I feel the same way.

MAN: But you live here—alone?

WOMAN: Yes.

MAN: It's so quiet here. How can you sleep?

WOMAN: Tonight, I'll sleep. I'll lie down in the next room, and hear your breathing through the wall, and fall asleep shamelessly. There will be no silence.

MAN: You're very kind to let me stay here.

WOMAN: This is yours. *(She unrolls a mat)*

MAN: Did you make it yourself?

WOMAN: Yes. There is a place to wash outside.

MAN: Thank you.

WOMAN: Good night.

MAN: Good night. *(He starts to leave)*

WOMAN: May I know your name?

MAN: No. I mean, I would rather not say. If I gave you a name, it would only be made up. Why should I deceive you? You are too kind for that.

WOMAN: Then what should I call you? Perhaps—"Man Who Fears Silence"?

MAN: How about, "Man Who Fears Women"?

WOMAN: That name is much too common.

MAN: And you?

WOMAN: Hanako.

MAN: That's your name?

WOMAN: It's what you may call me.

MAN: Good night, Hanako. You are very kind.

WOMAN: You are very smart. Good night.

(Man exits. Woman picks up the dishes and teapot, returns them offstage to kitchen. She goes to the vase. She picks up the flowers, studies them. She carries them out of the room with her. Man reenters. He glimpses the spot where the vase used to sit. He listens at the various screens, then suddenly hears a sound. He prepares to draw his sword, then hears a shakuhatchi. *He sits on the mat, looks at his flower, puts it away. Then he sits on guard with his sword ready at his side.)*

Scene Two

Dawn. Man is packing. Woman enters with food.

WOMAN: Good morning.

MAN: Good morning, Hanako.

WOMAN: You weren't planning to leave?

MAN: I have quite a distance to travel today.

WOMAN: Please. *(She offers him food)*

MAN: Thank you. *(He eats)*

WOMAN: May I ask where you're traveling to?

MAN: It's far.

WOMAN: I know this region well.

MAN: Oh? Do you leave the house often?

WOMAN: I used to. I used to travel a great deal. I know the region from those days.

MAN: You probably wouldn't know the place I'm headed.

WOMAN: Why not?

MAN: It's new. A new village. It didn't exist in "those days."

(Pause.)

WOMAN: I thought you said you wouldn't deceive me.

MAN: I didn't. You don't believe me, do you?

WOMAN: No.

MAN: Then I didn't deceive you, did I? I'm traveling. That much is true.

WOMAN: Are you in such a hurry?

MAN: Traveling is a matter of timing. Catching the light.

(Woman exits. Man finishes eating, puts down his bowl. Woman reenters with the vase of flowers.)

Where did you find those? They don't grow native around these parts, do they?

WOMAN: No, they've all been brought in by visitors. Such as yourself. They were left here. In my custody.

MAN: But—they look so fresh, so alive.

WOMAN: I take care of them. They remind me of the people and places outside this house.

MAN: May I touch them?

WOMAN: Certainly.

MAN: These have just blossomed.

WOMAN: No, they were in bloom yesterday. If you'd noticed them before, you would know that.

MAN: You must have received these very recently. I would guess—within five days.

WOMAN: I don't know. But I wouldn't trust your estimate. It's all in the amount of care you show to them. I create a world which is outside the realm of what you know.

MAN: What do you do?

WOMAN: I can't explain. Words are too inefficient. It takes hundreds of words to describe a single act of caring. With hundreds of acts, words become irrelevant. *(Pause)* But perhaps you can stay.

MAN: How long?

WOMAN: As long as you'd like.

MAN: Why?

WOMAN: To see how I care for them.

MAN: I *am* tired.

WOMAN: Rest.

MAN: The light?

WOMAN: It will return.

Scene Three

Day. Man is carrying chopped wood. He is stripped to the waist. Woman enters.

WOMAN: You're very kind to do that for me.

MAN: I enjoy it, you know. Chopping wood. It's clean. No questions. You take your ax, you stand up the log, you aim—pow!—you either hit it or you don't. Success or failure.

WOMAN: You seem to have been very successful today.

MAN: Why shouldn't I be? It's a beautiful day. I can see to those hills. The trees are cool. The sun is gentle. Ideal. If a man can't be successful on a day like this, he might as well kick the dust up into his own face.

(Man notices Woman staring at him. Man pats his belly, looks at her.)

Protection from falls.

WOMAN: What?

(Man touches his belly, showing some fat.)

Oh. Don't be silly.

(Man begins slapping the fat on his belly to a rhythm.)

MAN: Listen—I can make music—see? That wasn't always possible. But now—that I've developed this—whenever I need entertainment . . . *(He continues slapping)*

WOMAN: You shouldn't make fun of your body.

MAN: Why not? I saw you. You were staring.

WOMAN: I wasn't making fun. I was just—stop that!

(He stops.)

MAN: Then why were you staring?

WOMAN: I was . . .

MAN: Laughing?

WOMAN: No.

MAN: Well?

WOMAN: I was—your body. It's . . . strong.

(Pause.)

MAN: People say that. But they don't know. I've heard that age brings wisdom. That's a laugh. The years don't accumulate here. They accumulate here. *(He pats his stomach)* But today is a day to be happy, right? The woods. The sun. Blue. It's a happy day. I'm going to chop wood.

WOMAN: There's nothing left to chop. Look.

MAN: Oh. I guess . . . that's it.

WOMAN: Sit. Here.

MAN: But . . .

WOMAN: There's nothing left. Learn to love it.

MAN: Don't be ridiculous.

WOMAN: Touch it.

MAN: It's flabby.

WOMAN: It's strong.

MAN: It's weak.

WOMAN: And smooth.

MAN: Do you mind if I put on my shirt?

WOMAN: Of course not. Shall I get it for you?

MAN: No. No. Just sit there. (*Picks up his shirt. He pauses, studies his body*) You think it's cute, huh?

WOMAN: I think you should learn to love it.

(*Man pats his belly.*)

MAN (*To belly*): You're okay, sir. You hang onto my body like a great horseman.

WOMAN: Not like that.

MAN (*Still to belly*): You're also faithful. You'll never leave me for another man.

WOMAN: No.

MAN: What do you want me to say?

(*Woman leans over to Man. She touches his belly with her hand.*)

Scene Four

Night. Man is alone. Flowers are gone from stand. Mat is unrolled. Man lies on it, sleeping. Suddenly, he starts, awakened by the sound of the shakuhatchi. *He sits up and grabs his sword, then relaxes as he recognizes the instrument. He crosses to a screen and listens, then returns to the mat and sits. He takes out the stolen flower. He stares into it.*

Scene Five

Day. Woman is cleaning while Man exercises. She is on her hands and knees, scrubbing the floor.

MAN: I heard your playing last night.
WOMAN: My playing?
MAN: *Shakuhatchi.*
WOMAN: Oh.
MAN: You played very softly. I had to strain to hear it. Next time don't be afraid. Play out. Fully. Clear. It must've been very beautiful, if only I could've heard it clearly. Why don't you play for me sometime?
WOMAN: I'm very shy about it.
MAN: Why?
WOMAN: I play for my own satisfaction. That's all. It's something I developed on my own. I don't know if it's at all acceptable by outside standards.
MAN: Play for me. I'll tell you.
WOMAN: No, I'm sure you're too knowledgeable in the arts.
MAN: Who? Me?
WOMAN: You being from the city and all.
MAN: I'm ignorant, believe me.
WOMAN: I'd play, and you'd probably bite your cheek.
MAN: Ask me a question about music. Any question. I'll answer incorrectly. I guarantee it.
WOMAN *(Looking at the floor)*: Look at this.
MAN: What?
WOMAN: A stain.
MAN: Where?
WOMAN: Here? See? I can't get it out.
MAN: Oh. I hadn't noticed it before.
WOMAN: I notice it every time I clean.
MAN: Here. Let me try.
WOMAN: Thank you.
MAN: Ugh. It's tough.

WOMAN: I know.

MAN: How did it get here?

WOMAN: It's been there as long as I've lived here.

MAN: I hardly stand a chance. *(Pause)* But I'll try. *(He begins to scrub)* One—two—three—four! One—two—three—four! See, you set up . . . gotta set up . . . a rhythm—two—three—four. Used to practice with a rhythm. One—two—three—four. Yes, remember. Like battle . . . like fighting, one—two—three—four. One—two—three—four. Look . . . there it goes . . . got the sides . . . the edges . . . fading away . . . fading quick . . . toward the center to the heart . . . two—three—four. One—two—three—four—dead!

WOMAN: Dead.

MAN: I got it! I got it! A little rhythm! All it took! Four! Four!

WOMAN: Thank you.

MAN: I didn't think I could do it . . . but there—it's gone—I did it!

WOMAN: Yes. You did.

MAN: And you—you were great.

WOMAN: No—I just watched.

MAN: We were a team! You and me!

WOMAN: I only provided encouragement.

MAN: You were great! You were!

(Man grabs Woman. Pause.)

WOMAN: It's gone. Thank you. Would you like to hear me play *shakuhatchi*?

MAN: Yes I would.

WOMAN: I don't usually play for visitors. It's so . . . I'm not sure. I developed it—all by myself—in times when I was alone. I heard nothing . . . The air began to be oppressive—stale. So I learned to play *shakuhatchi*. I learned to make sounds on it. I tried to make these sounds resemble the human voice. The *shakuhatchi* became my weapon. It kept me from choking on many a silent evening.

MAN: I'm here. You can hear my voice.
WOMAN: Speak again.
MAN: I will.

Scene Six

Night. Man is sleeping. Suddenly, he starts. He lifts his head up. He listens. The shakuhatchi *melody rises up once more. This time, however, it becomes louder and more clear than before. He gets up. He cannot tell from what direction the music is coming. It seems to come from all directions at once, as omnipresent as the air. Slowly, he moves toward a sliding panel through which the woman enters and exits. He puts his ear against it, thinking the music may be coming from there. Slowly, he slides the door open just a crack, ever so carefully. He peeks through the crack. As he peeks through, the upstage wall of the set becomes transparent, and through the scrim, we are able to see what he sees. Woman is upstage of the scrim. She is carrying the vase of flowers in front of her as she moves slowly upstage of the scrim. She is transformed; she is beautiful. She wears a brightly colored kimono. Man observes this scene for a long time. He then slides the door shut. The scrim returns to opaque. The music continues. He returns to his mat. He picks up the stolen flower. It is brown and wilted, dead. He looks at it, throws it down. The music slowly fades out.*

Scene Seven

Morning. Man is practicing sword maneuvers. He practices with the feel of a man whose spirit is willing but flesh is inept. He tries to execute deft movements but is dissatisfied with his efforts. Suddenly, he feels something buzzing around his neck—a mosquito. He slaps his neck, but misses it. He sees it flying near him. He swipes at it with his sword. He keeps missing. Finally, he thinks he's hit it. He runs over, kneels down to recover the fallen insect. He picks up the two halves of the mosquito on two different fingers. Woman enters the room. She again looks as she normally does. She is carrying the vase of flowers, which she places on its shelf.

MAN: Look.
WOMAN: I'm sorry?
MAN: Look.
WOMAN: What?

    (He brings over the two halves of the mosquito to show her.)

MAN: See?
WOMAN: Oh.
MAN: I hit it—chop!
WOMAN: These are new forms of target practice?
MAN: Huh? Well—yes—in a way.
WOMAN: You seem to do well at it.
MAN: Thank you. For last night. I heard your *shakuhatchi*. It was very loud, strong—good tone.
WOMAN: Did you enjoy it? I wanted you to enjoy it. If you wish, I'll play it for you every night.
MAN: Every night!
WOMAN: If you wish.
MAN: No—I don't—I don't want you to treat me like a baby.
WOMAN: What? I'm not.
MAN: Oh, yes. Like a baby who you must feed in the middle of the night or he cries. Waaah! Waaah!
WOMAN: Stop that!
MAN: You need your sleep.
WOMAN: I don't mind getting up for you. *(Pause)* I would enjoy playing for you. Every night. While you sleep. It will make me feel . . . like I'm shaping your dreams. I go through long stretches when there is no one in my dreams. It's terrible. During those times, I avoid my bed as much as possible. I paint. I weave. I play

shakuhatchi. I sit on mats and rub powder into my face. Anything to keep from facing a bed with no dreams. It is like sleeping on ice.

MAN: What do you dream of now?

WOMAN: Last night—I dreamt of you. I don't remember what happened. But you were very funny. Not in a mocking way. I wasn't laughing at you. But you made me laugh. And you were very warm. I remember that. *(Pause)* What do you remember about last night?

MAN: Just your playing. That's all. I got up, listened to it, and went back to sleep. *(Resumes practicing with his sword)*

WOMAN: Another mosquito bothering you?

MAN: Just practicing. Ah! Weak! Too weak! I tell you, it wasn't always like this. I'm telling you, there were days when I could chop the fruit from a tree without ever taking my eyes off the ground. *(Continuing to practice with his sword)* You ever use one of these?

WOMAN: I've had to pick one up, yes.

MAN: Oh?

WOMAN: You forget . . . I live alone . . . out here . . . there is . . . not much to sustain me but what I manage to learn myself. It wasn't really a matter of choice.

MAN: I used to be very good, you know. Perhaps I can give you some pointers.

WOMAN: I'd really rather not.

MAN: C'mon—a woman like you—you're absolutely right. You need to know how to defend yourself.

WOMAN: As you wish.

MAN: Do you have something to practice with?

WOMAN: Yes. Excuse me. *(She exits. She reenters with two wooden sticks)* Will these do?

MAN: Fine. *(He takes one)* Nice. Now, show me what you can do.

WOMAN: I'm sorry?

MAN: Run up and hit me.

WOMAN: Please.

MAN: Go on—I'll block it.

WOMAN: I feel so . . . undignified.
MAN: Go on!

(She taps him playfully.)

Not like that! C'mon!
WOMAN: I'll try to be gentle.
MAN: What?
WOMAN: I don't want to hurt you.
MAN: You won't. Hit me!

(Woman charges at Man, quickly, deftly. She scores a hit.)

WOMAN: Did I hurt you? I'm sorry.
MAN: No.
WOMAN: I hurt you.
MAN: Don't be ridiculous!
WOMAN: Do you wish to hit me?
MAN: No.
WOMAN: Do you want me to try again?
MAN: No. Just practice there—by yourself—let me see you run through some maneuvers.
WOMAN: Must I?
MAN: Yes! Go!

(Woman goes to an open area.)

My greatest strength always was as a teacher.

(Woman executes a series of movements with great skill and fierceness. Her whole manner is transformed. Man watches with increasing amazement. Her movements end. She regains her submissive manner.)

WOMAN: I'm so embarrassed. My skills—they're so—inappropriate. I look like a man.
MAN: Where did you learn that?
WOMAN: There is much time to practice here.
MAN: But you—the techniques . . .
WOMAN: I don't know what's fashionable in the outside world. *(Pause)* Are you unhappy?

MAN: No.

WOMAN: Really?

MAN: I'm just . . . surprised.

WOMAN: You think it's unbecoming for a woman.

MAN: No, no. Not at all.

WOMAN: You want to leave.

MAN: No!

WOMAN: All visitors do. I know. I've met many. They say they'll stay. And they do. For a while. Until they see too much. Or they learn something new. There are boundaries outside of which visitors do not want to see me step. Only who knows what those boundaries are? Not I. They change with every visitor. You have to be careful not to cross them, but you never know where they are. And one day, inevitably, you step outside the lines. The visitor knows. You don't. You didn't know that you'd done anything different. You thought it was just another part of you. The visitor sneaks away. The next day, you learn that you had stepped outside his heart. I'm afraid you've seen too much.

MAN: There are stories.

WOMAN: What?

MAN: People talk.

WOMAN: Where? We're two days from the nearest village.

MAN: Word travels.

WOMAN: What are you talking about?

MAN: There are stories about you. I heard them. They say that your visitors never leave this house.

WOMAN: That's what you heard?

MAN: They say you imprison them.

WOMAN: Then you were a fool to come here.

MAN: Listen.

WOMAN: Me? Listen? You. Look! Where are these prisoners? Have you seen any?

MAN: They told me you were very beautiful.

WOMAN: Then they are blind as well as ignorant.

MAN: You are.

WOMAN: What?

MAN: Beautiful.

WOMAN: Stop that! My skin feels like seaweed.

MAN: I didn't realize it at first. I must confess. I didn't. But over these few days—your face has changed for me. The shape of it. The feel of it. The color. All changed. I look at you now and I am no longer sure you are the same woman who had poured tea for me just a week ago. And because of that I remember—how little I know about a face that changes in the night. *(Pause)* Have you heard those stories?

WOMAN: I don't listen to old wives' tales.

MAN: But have you heard them?

WOMAN: Yes. I've heard them. From other visitors— young—hot-blooded—or old—who came here because they were told great glory was to be had by killing the witch in the woods.

MAN: I was told that no man could spend time in this house without falling in love.

WOMAN: Oh? So why did you come? Did you wager gold that you could come out untouched? The outside world is so flattering to me. And you—are you like the rest? Passion passing through your heart so powerfully that you can't hold onto it?

MAN: No! I'm afraid.

WOMAN: Of what?

MAN: Sometimes—when I look into the flowers, I think I hear a voice—from inside—a voice beneath the petals. A human voice.

WOMAN: What does it say? "Let me out"?

MAN: No. Listen. It hums. It hums with the peacefulness of one who is completely imprisoned.

WOMAN: I understand that if you listen closely enough, you can hear the ocean.

MAN: No. Wait. Look at it. *(He takes a flower from the vase)* See the layers? Each petal—hiding the next. Try and see where they end . . . You can't. Follow them down, further down, around and as you come down—faster and faster—the breeze picks up. The breeze becomes a wail. And in that rush of air—you can hear a voice.

(Woman grabs flower from Man.)

WOMAN: So, you believe I water and prune my lovers? How can you be so foolish? *(She throws the flower to the ground)* Do you come only to leave again? To take a chunk of my heart, then leave with your booty on your belt, like a prize? You say that I imprison hearts in these flowers? Well, bits of my heart are trapped with travelers across this land. I can't even keep track. So kill me. If you came here to destroy a witch, kill me now. I can't stand to have it happen again.

(Man begins to pull out sword, but stops—he cannot use it.)

MAN: I won't leave you.
WOMAN: I believe you.

Scene Eight

Day. Woman is modeling a kimono.

WOMAN: Do you like it?
MAN: Yes, it's beautiful.
WOMAN: I wanted to wear something special today.
MAN: It's beautiful. *(He takes out his sword)* Excuse me. I must practice.
WOMAN: Shall I get you something?
MAN: No.
WOMAN: Some tea, maybe?
MAN: No, thank you. *(He resumes swordplay)*
WOMAN: Perhaps later today—perhaps we can go out—just around here. We can look for flowers.
MAN: All right.

WOMAN: We don't have to.

MAN: No. Let's.

WOMAN: I just thought if . . .

MAN: Fine. Where do you want to go?

WOMAN: There are very few recreational activities around here, I know.

MAN: All right. We'll go this afternoon.

(*Pause.*)

WOMAN: Can I get you something?

MAN: What?

WOMAN: You might be . . .

MAN: I'm not hungry or thirsty or cold or hot.

WOMAN: Then what are you?

MAN: Practicing.

(*Man resumes practicing; Woman exits. Man sits down. He examines his sword, thinks. He stands up. He places the sword on the ground with the tip pointed directly upward. He keeps the sword from falling by placing the tip under his chin. He experiments with different degrees of pressure. Woman reenters. She sees him in this precarious position.*)

WOMAN: Don't do that!

MAN: What?

WOMAN: You can hurt yourself!

MAN: I was practicing!

WOMAN: You were playing!

MAN: I was practicing!

WOMAN: It's dangerous.

MAN: What do you take me for—a child?

WOMAN: Sometimes wise men do childish things.

MAN: I knew what I was doing!

WOMAN: It scares me.

MAN: Don't be ridiculous.

WOMAN: Don't! Don't do that!

MAN: Get back!

WOMAN: But . . .

MAN: Ssssh!

WOMAN: I wish . . .

MAN: Listen to me! The slightest shock, you know—the slightest shock—surprise—it might make me jerk or—something—and then . . . So you must be perfectly still and quiet.

WOMAN: But I . . .

MAN: Ssssh!

(Silence, then . . .)

I learned this exercise from a friend—I can't even remember his name—good swordsman—many years ago. He called it his meditation position. He said, like this, he could feel the line between this world and the others because he rested on it. If he saw something in another world that he liked better, all he would have to do is let his head drop, and he'd be there. Simple. No fuss. One day, they found him with the tip of his sword run clean out the back of his neck. He was smiling. I guess he saw something he liked. Or else he'd fallen asleep.

WOMAN: Stop that.

MAN: Stop what?

WOMAN: Tormenting me.

MAN: I'm not.

WOMAN: Take it away!

MAN: You don't have to watch, you know.

WOMAN: Do you want to die that way—an accident?

MAN: I was doing this before you came in.

WOMAN: If you do, all you need to do is tell me.

MAN: What?

WOMAN: I can walk right over. Lean on the back of your head.

MAN: Don't try to threaten . . .

WOMAN: Or jerk your sword up.

MAN: . . . or scare me. You can't threaten . . .

WOMAN: I'm not. But if that's what you want.

MAN: You wouldn't do it.

WOMAN: Oh?

MAN: Then I'd be gone. You wouldn't let me leave that easily.

WOMAN: Yes, I would.

MAN: You'd be alone.

WOMAN: No. I'd follow you. Forever. *(Pause)* Now, let's stop this nonsense.

MAN: No! I can do what I want! Don't come any closer!

WOMAN: Then release your sword.

MAN: Come any closer and I'll drop my head.

> *(Woman slowly approaches Man. She grabs the sword. She pulls it out from under his chin.)*

WOMAN: There will be no more of this.

> *(She exits with the sword. He starts to follow her, then stops. He touches under his chin. On his finger, he finds a drop of blood.)*

Scene Nine

Night. Man, wearing a coat and carrying a bundle of his possessions, is leaving the house. Woman appears in the doorway to the outside.

WOMAN: It's time for you to go?

MAN: Yes. I'm sorry.

WOMAN: You're just going to sneak out? A thief in the night? A frightened child?

MAN: I care about you.

WOMAN: You express it strangely.

MAN: I leave in shame because it is proper. *(Pause)* I came seeking glory.

WOMAN: To kill me? You can say it. You'll be surprised at how little I blanch. As if you'd said, "I came for a bowl of rice," or "I came seeking love," or "I came to kill you."

MAN: Weakness. All weakness. Too weak to kill you. Too weak to kill myself. Too weak to do anything but sneak away in shame.

173

(Woman brings out Man's sword.)

WOMAN: Were you even planning to leave without this?

(He takes sword.)

Why not stay here?

MAN: I can't live with someone who's defeated me.

WOMAN: I never thought of defeating you. I only wanted to take care of you. To make you happy. Because that made me happy and I was no longer alone.

MAN: You defeated me.

WOMAN: Why do you think that way?

MAN: I came here with a purpose. The world was clear. You changed the shape of your face, the shape of my heart—rearranged everything—created a world where I could do nothing.

WOMAN: I only tried to care for you.

MAN: I guess that was all it took.

(Pause.)

WOMAN: You still think I'm a witch. Just because old women gossip. You are so cruel. Once you arrived, there were only two possibilities: I would die or you would leave. *(Pause)* If you believe I'm a witch, then kill me. Rid the province of one more evil.

MAN: I can't—

WOMAN: Why not? If you believe that about me, then it's the right thing to do.

MAN: You know I can't.

WOMAN: Then stay.

MAN: Don't try to force me!

WOMAN: I won't force you to do anything. *(Pause)* All I wanted was an escape—for both of us. The sound of a human voice—the simplest thing to find, and the hardest to hold on to. This house—my loneliness is etched into the walls. Kill me, but don't leave. Even in death, my spirit would rest here and be comforted by your presence.

MAN: Force me to stay.

WOMAN: I won't.

(Man starts to leave.)

Beware.

MAN: Of what?

WOMAN: The ground on which you walk is weak. It could give way at any moment. The crevice beneath is dark.

MAN: Are you talking about death? I'm ready to die.

WOMAN: Fear for what is worse than death.

MAN: What?

WOMAN: Falling. Falling through the darkness. Waiting to hit the ground. Picking up speed. Waiting for the ground. Falling faster. Falling alone. Waiting. Falling. Waiting. Falling.

(Man exits. Woman goes out through the door to her room. After a long beat, he reenters. He looks for her in the main room. He goes to the mat, sees her shakuhatchi. He puts down his sword, takes off his bundle and coat. He goes inside. He comes out. He goes to the mat, picks up her shakuhatchi, clutches it to him. He moves everything else off the mat, sits and puts the shakuhatchi to his mouth. He begins to blow into it. He tries to make sounds. He continues trying through the end of the play.

The upstage scrim lights up. Upstage, we see the woman. She has hung herself and is hanging from a rope suspended from the roof. Around her swirl thousands of petals from the flowers. They fill the upstage scrim area like a blizzard of color.

Man continues to attempt to play. Lights fade to black.)

END OF PLAY

THE HOUSE
OF SLEEPING
BEAUTIES
(1983)

Adapted from the short story by
Yasunari Kawabata

To Natolie

Production History

The House of Sleeping Beauties opened with *The Sound of a Voice* under the title *Sound and Beauty* at The Joseph Papp Public Theater/New York Shakespeare Festival (Joseph Papp, Producer), in New York City on November 6, 1983. It was directed by John Lone and assisted by Lenore Kletter; the set design was by Andrew Jackness; the costume design was by Lydia Tanji; the lighting design was by John Gisondi; and the music was by Lucia Hwong. There was also a dancer, Elizabeth Fong Sung, in this production. The cast was as follows:

WOMAN   Ching Valdes
KAWABATA   Victor Wong

Characters

WOMAN, Japanese, late seventies.
YASUNARI Kawabata, a leading Japanese novelist, seventy-
  two.

Place

The sitting room of the House of Sleeping Beauties, Tokyo.

Time

1972.

Scene One: night.
Scene Two: the following evening.
Scene Three: several months later, evening.
Scene Four: one week later, evening.

Definitions

bon-odori is a festival dance.
hara-kiri is a ritual suicide.
koto is a zither-like Japanese musical instrument.
sensei is a revered teacher.
Shifuno Tomo is a popular magazine.

Playwright's Note

This play is a fantasy. In historical fact, Kawabata's composition of his novelette *House of the Sleeping Beauties* and his unexplained suicide occurred many years apart.

Many people helped me develop this play, and I'd like to thank especially Grafton Mouen, Jean Brody, John Harnagel, Marcy Mattox, Natolie Miyawaki, Nancy Takahashi, Mitch Motooka and Helen Merrill.

Scene One

A sitting room. Not richly decorated. Desk, pillows, low table, equipment for tea, cabinet, screen, mirror, stove. It is night. Woman sits at desk, writing. Kawabata paces.

WOMAN: Now, you mustn't do anything distasteful.

KAWABATA: Distasteful?

WOMAN: You mustn't stick your fingers in the girl's mouth or anything like that.

KAWABATA: Oh, no. I wouldn't think of it.

WOMAN: Good. All my guests are gentlemen.

KAWABATA: Would you please put that down?

WOMAN *(Indicating the pen)*: This?

KAWABATA: Yes. I'm not here to be interviewed.

WOMAN: Perhaps. *I* am, however, accountable to my girls—

KAWABATA: Fine.

WOMAN: —and must therefore ask a few questions of those who wish to become my guests.

KAWABATA: You assume too easily, madame.

WOMAN: Oh?

KAWABATA: You assume that my presence here identifies me as just one type of man.

WOMAN: On the contrary, sir.

KAWABATA: Why did you assume I was going in there, then?

WOMAN: I never assumed any such thing. Did you assume I was going to allow you in there?

(Pause.)

KAWABATA: "Allow me"?

WOMAN: Actually, I identify two types of men, sir—gentlemen and those who do not behave. My guests are all gentlemen. They do not disgrace the house. Obviously, very few men meet these requirements.

KAWABATA: What are you talking about?

WOMAN: I must protect my girls—and the house.

KAWABATA: Well, I mean, I'm certainly not going to assault a girl, if that's what you mean. Is that what you think? That I look like a man who goes to brothels?

WOMAN: Neither looks nor brothels has much to do with it, sir. My experience has taught me that in most cases if you scratch a man you'll find a molester.

KAWABATA: Well, if you take that kind of attitude . . .

WOMAN: A look in most men's bottom drawers confirms this.

KAWABATA: . . . how is any man to prove he's a . . . a gentleman, as you say?

WOMAN: I take a risk on all my guests. But I have my methods; I judge as best I can.

KAWABATA: That's ridiculous. That men must be . . . tested to become your customers. But all your customers are practically ghosts anyway—of course they don't object. Their throats are too dry to protest.

WOMAN: Guests.

KAWABATA: I'm sorry?

WOMAN: They're not customers, they're guests.

KAWABATA: Well, I, for one, do not intend to become a guest, understand?

WOMAN: You are very proud.

KAWABATA: Proud?

WOMAN: But that doesn't necessarily mean you are not a gentleman. Sometimes the proudest men are the best behaved. So, you don't want to be my guest. What *do* you want?

KAWABATA: I only want to talk.

WOMAN: About what?

KAWABATA: Your house.

WOMAN: Window shopping?

KAWABATA: No.

WOMAN: I'm sorry.

KAWABATA: I want to know why the old men come here.

WOMAN: But all your answers are in there.

KAWABATA: No, they're not. I could never feel what they feel, what brings them back—a parade of corpses—night after night. But you—perhaps they share their secrets.

WOMAN: I have no secrets.

KAWABATA: Old Eguchi—

WOMAN: And I'm no gossip.

KAWABATA: He talked to me last week.

WOMAN: Yes, he called and said you were coming.

KAWABATA: Said he comes here almost every night. I wanted him to tell me more, but he said I could only know more by talking to you.

WOMAN: He said you wished to gain entrance.

KAWABATA: No—he's making the same mistake as you. I won't be able to feel what he feels because my mind's different.

WOMAN: Oh?

KAWABATA: Eguchi's so old.

WOMAN: And you're young?

KAWABATA: Well, no. Not in years.

WOMAN: Oh.

KAWABATA: But my mind is young. Eguchi's is gone. He sits on his futon each afternoon swatting bees with tissue paper. Listen, I know you're a woman of business— may I offer you some fee for what you know?

WOMAN: Money?

KAWABATA: Don't worry. I'm not with the police or anything.

WOMAN: Don't be ridiculous. What do you take me for?

KAWABATA: What do I—?

WOMAN: You might as well pay me to tell you how one falls in love.

KAWABATA: What do you take yourself for, madame—acting like a sorceress, a *sensei*. You're just an old woman running this house. I have questions, and I'm willing to pay for the answers.

WOMAN: I have questions also. Fair, sir? *(Pause)* How old are you?

KAWABATA: I won't answer just anything, you know.

WOMAN: Don't worry. Neither will I.

KAWABATA: Seventy-two.

WOMAN: Married?

KAWABATA: My wife passed away . . . several years ago.

WOMAN: I'm sorry. Children?

KAWABATA: Yes. Two. Daughters. Why are you asking this?

WOMAN: Don't worry. I'm no gossip. Retired?

KAWABATA: Uh—no . . . I mean, yes.

WOMAN: Yes or no?

KAWABATA: Uh—no.

WOMAN: No? No. Profession?

KAWABATA: Uh—teacher.

WOMAN: Teacher.

KAWABATA: University level, of course.

WOMAN: There. That wasn't so bad, was it?

KAWABATA: That's all?

WOMAN: Now, what would *you* like to know?

KAWABATA: From that, you decide?

WOMAN: I *would* like you to join me in a game, though.

KAWABATA: A game?

WOMAN: Yes. And as we play, we can talk about the rooms. Do you mind?

KAWABATA: Well, if it's harmless.

WOMAN: Quite. Would you like some tea?

KAWABATA: Oh, yes. Please. Thank you. This game—what's it called?

WOMAN: I don't know. It's old. Geishas used to play it with their customers, to relax them. *(She brings the tea, pours it)*

KAWABATA: Relax? Perhaps it will relax me. *(He laughs softly)* Now, why do you want me to play this?

(Woman pulls a box out of the desk and opens it. Inside are twenty-five smooth tiles, five times as long as they are wide. While she speaks, she stacks them in five layers of five tiles each, such that the tiles of each layer are perpendicular to those of the layer below it.)

WOMAN: So we can get to know each other. As I said, I must protect my girls from men who do not behave.

KAWABATA: You talk as if men should be put on leashes.

WOMAN: No, leashes aren't necessary at all. *(She finishes the tower)* There. We'll take turns removing tiles from the tower until it collapses. Understand?

KAWABATA: Is this a game you ask all your customers to play?

WOMAN: Guests. You can't touch the top layer, though, and you can only use one hand.

KAWABATA: But what's the object? Who wins, who loses?

WOMAN: There are no winners or losers. There is only the tower—intact or collapsed. Just one hand—like this. *(She removes a piece)*

KAWABATA: My turn? What am I trying to do?

WOMAN: Judge the tiles. Wriggle that one, for instance— yes, that one you're touching—between your fingers. Is the weight of the stack on it? If so, don't force it. Leave it and look for another one that's looser. If you try to force the tiles to be what they're not, the whole thing will come crashing down.

KAWABATA: A test of skills? There— *(He removes a piece)* Your turn.

WOMAN: See? Simple.

KAWABATA: What kind of a test—? You're just an old woman. What kind of a contest is this?

WOMAN: Let's talk about you, sir. We want to make you happy.

(They continue to take turns removing tiles throughout the following section.)

KAWABATA: Happy? No, you don't understand. You can't—
WOMAN: Our guests sleep much better here. It's the warmth, they say.
KAWABATA: I don't have any trouble sleeping.
WOMAN: Don't you?
KAWABATA: Sometimes . . . sometimes I choose not to go to bed. But when I do, I sleep.
WOMAN: Our guests are never afraid to go to sleep.
KAWABATA: It's not that I'm afraid.
WOMAN: The darkness does not threaten them.

(Pause.)

KAWABATA: Old Eguchi—he says that the girls . . . that they are naked.
WOMAN: Yes.
KAWABATA: He says they are very beautiful, but I hardly . . .
WOMAN: For you, I would pick an especially pretty one.
KAWABATA: For me—? Don't start—
WOMAN: How old was your wife when you first met her?
KAWABATA: My wife? Oh, I don't know. She must have been—oh, maybe nineteen.
WOMAN: Nineteen. That is a beautiful age. I would pick one who is nineteen.
KAWABATA: Don't be ridiculous. She'd see me and—
WOMAN: But you forget, sir—our girls won't see anything.
KAWABATA: I suppose you have some way of guaranteeing this. I suppose it's never happened that some girl has opened her eyes—
WOMAN: No. Never.

(Kawabata is having a particularly difficult time with a tile.)

KAWABATA: Look at this. *(He holds out his hand, laughs)* Shaking. Would you mind putting some more wood in the furnace?
WOMAN: Of course. *(She rises to do so as she talks)* I know what girl I would pick for you. She is half Japanese,

half Caucasian. She has the most delicate hair—brown in one light, black in another. As she sleeps, she wriggles her left foot, like a cat, against the mattress, as if to draw out even the last bits of warmth.

(Woman returns to the table, sits. As she does, Kawabata removes a tile and causes the tower to fall.)

KAWABATA: Ai! You shook it.
WOMAN: No.

(During the next section, Woman gets up, goes to the cabinet, removes a small jar filled with clear liquid and a tiny cup. She pours the liquid into the cup.)

KAWABATA: Maybe an accident, but still—
WOMAN: I assure you.
KAWABATA: —when you sat down.
WOMAN: I was perfectly still.
KAWABATA: No, you shook the table.
WOMAN: I didn't touch it.
KAWABATA: Just a bit.
WOMAN: Really.
KAWABATA: But at the crucial moment.
WOMAN: Please, sir.
KAWABATA: Just as it was about to give.
WOMAN: Thank you for playing.
KAWABATA: It wasn't fair.
WOMAN: Please—
KAWABATA: It was my first time.
WOMAN: —take this cup.
KAWABATA: What?
WOMAN: Here.

(He takes it.)

KAWABATA: What is this?
WOMAN: To help you sleep.
KAWABATA: Sleep?

WOMAN: To assure you a restful evening—in there. *(Pause)* If you wish to, you may now go in. You're my guest. If you still have questions after tonight, I'll try to answer some—

KAWABATA: I can just—

WOMAN: —on your next visit.

KAWABATA: —go in?

WOMAN: Welcome. Your name?

KAWABATA: My name?

WOMAN: We keep names of all our guests.

KAWABATA: But I don't see why . . .

WOMAN: Our guests are our friends. Sometimes we like to let our friends know if we have something special. Don't worry, it is confidential.

KAWABATA: Kawabata. *(He drinks from the cup)*

WOMAN: May I help you undress, Mr. Kawabata?

KAWABATA: Oh, yes. Thank you.

(They go behind the screen.)

I can just . . . go in?

WOMAN: Yes. On the right, second door. *(Pause)* She's a very pretty girl.

KAWABATA: Second door.

WOMAN: On the right. She's asleep, waiting for you.

(She gives him a key. Pause.)

KAWABATA: I'm really only curious.

WOMAN: I know. That's why you should go in.

KAWABATA: What if . . . something happens?

WOMAN: Something?

KAWABATA: What if she wakes up?

WOMAN: Even if you were to try your utmost—you could cut off her arms and she wouldn't wake up 'til morning. Don't worry.

(They come out from behind the screen. He wears a light robe.)

Sleep well, Mr. Kawabata. A boy will wake you and
bring you tea in the morning.

KAWABATA: Uh—thank you.

(She opens the door.)

WOMAN: Listen.

KAWABATA: Listen?

WOMAN: To the waves. And the wind.

(Silence.)

Good night, Mr. Kawabata.

*(He walks through the door; she closes it. She moves to the
table, begins cleaning up the tiles, as lights fade to black.)*

Scene Two

*It is the following evening. In the darkness, we see a flame.
Then, the lights come up. Woman sits at the desk. Kawabata is
burning his record from yesterday; he tosses it into the stove.*

KAWABATA: I'm not a teacher, madame. I'm a writer.

WOMAN: Oh. A writer?

KAWABATA: Have you read my novels, short stories?

WOMAN: Have you ever been published in this? *(She holds
up a magazine)*

KAWABATA: *Shifuno Tomo?* Trash.

WOMAN: Then I haven't read you.

KAWABATA: I don't write about beauty tips *or* American
movie stars.

WOMAN: So you're going to write a report on us.

KAWABATA: I'm not a reporter. I write stories, novels. For
some time now, I've been thinking about old men.
How it must—

WOMAN: If you wish to write your report, Mr. Kawabata,
you must realize the consequences of your actions. You

understand, don't you, that we can't let the outside know we're here. That would mean the end of the house.

KAWABATA: And that should worry me?

WOMAN: Does it? Didn't you sleep well?

KAWABATA: Hardly. I was afraid to touch the covers and disturb her. I studied the walls until I fell asleep, watched the colors change in the dark.

WOMAN: I see.

KAWABATA: But what I've learned about the state to which men come—to think they return—night after night—for that.

WOMAN: Then why have *you* returned?

KAWABATA: Me?

WOMAN: Why didn't you just write your report and destroy the house?

KAWABATA: Story. I wanted . . . to burn that.

WOMAN: Is that all?

KAWABATA: Yes. That's all. *(He chuckles)* I certainly have no desire to repeat last night's experience. It's been so many years since I've had to share a bed. No room to stretch.

WOMAN: Well, then, go.

KAWABATA: What?

WOMAN: If you've done what you've come for, then you must want to leave.

KAWABATA: Yes. I will. But first, I thought I might talk . . . to you.

WOMAN: What about? You've burned your record, you're no longer a guest, you plan to write your report without concern for the house, my girls, or myself.

KAWABATA: Yourself?

WOMAN: Our relationship is hardly suited to polite conversation.

KAWABATA: You will be all right.

WOMAN: "All right"? How can you be so insensitive? You talk like a man who lives in other men's beds.

KAWABATA: You are very defiant, madame. Defiance is admirable in a woman. Defiance in a man is nothing more than a trained response, since we always expect to get our way. But a woman's defiance is her own.

WOMAN: Mr. Kawabata, you must not write this report.

KAWABATA: What if I do?

WOMAN: Then my life is over.

KAWABATA: Don't be melodramatic.

WOMAN: Please. Don't talk of things you know nothing about. I can tell you. Only one other time—twenty years ago—have I ever misjudged a guest. He came back the next evening, as you have tonight, and informed me he was . . . with the authorities. Then he left. I didn't know what to do. First, I tried to imagine all the awful things that could happen, hoping that by picturing them, I would prevent them from taking place, since real life never happens like we envision it will. Finally, after an hour of this, I decided to sleep. As I lay in bed, I began to wonder, what else could I do? Where else could I go? I saw myself being carried up to Mount Obasute. My girls were carrying me up. "You're old now, Mama!" they cried. "We'll join your bones when we ourselves become old!" They left me in a cave and danced a *bon-odori* down the mountain, singing "Tokyo Ondo" as they went. (*She sings a little of it*) I thought, "Look at them dancing. That's why I'm here and they're leaving me. Anyone who can dance down the mountain is free to go." And the next thing I knew, I was dancing a *bon-odori* right up there, on my bed—the springs making the sounds young people make in beds. And I danced down the hall to a telephone and began looking for a new house for my girls. (*Pause*) That was twenty years ago. Look at me today. I can't even raise a foot for three seconds, let alone dance. I'm old, and I have no savings, no money, no skills. This time, Mr. Kawabata, I would have to stay on Mount Obasute.

KAWABATA: Look, madame, even if I wrote this story, it's possible that your house won't be affected.

WOMAN: Why? Don't people read them?

KAWABATA: Of course. But people will likely think it's all from my head. You haven't read my stories. Like what you said to me—"Listen to the waves," you said.

WOMAN: Yes, they often help men sleep.

KAWABATA: In one of my novels, the boy always makes love to the woman while listening to the waves. The critics would probably laugh—"Old Kawabata and waves. Can't he think of anything new?"

WOMAN: And if the authorities—some of whom already suspect our existence—if they read your story, that won't make them certain? *(Pause)* What is that story to you?

KAWABATA: I want to write this story. I can do it, I know. I haven't written a story in . . . in . . .

WOMAN: That's just one story to you. This is my life.

KAWABATA: Better if you were rid of it.

WOMAN: Then you must change the facts—

KAWABATA: You made a mistake, madame.

WOMAN: —to confuse the authorities.

KAWABATA: You chose not to cooperate with me yesterday.

WOMAN: But even that—

KAWABATA: You thought I was like the rest of them.

WOMAN: No, you mustn't write this report!

KAWABATA: You misjudged me. Now you see I'm different.

WOMAN: Yes, you are a reporter.

KAWABATA: You should have just told me about the house.

WOMAN: Mr. Kawabata—

KAWABATA: But you assumed—

WOMAN: —think of the girls.

KAWABATA: The girls?

WOMAN: The money they receive here.

KAWABATA: You shame them.

WOMAN: They are from poor families.

KAWABATA: They would be better off—

WOMAN: They come of their own will.

KAWABATA: —doing—working at . . . any other job.

WOMAN: And the old men.

KAWABATA: Don't tell me that.

WOMAN: We care about them. Look at this.

KAWABATA: At what?

WOMAN: At what you'll destroy.

KAWABATA: You humiliate them. Their despair—it's so great.

WOMAN: What do you know?

KAWABATA: Your girls—are they all still virgins?

WOMAN: Was yours?

KAWABATA: Yes. Do you see the depth of the old men's despair?

WOMAN: How do you know?

KAWABATA: That they can't even find the manhood to—

WOMAN: Mr. Kawabata, how do you know she was still a virgin?

(Pause.)

KAWABATA: Don't worry. I didn't . . . molest her. I walked into the room. I didn't believe she was going to be naked. I knew you'd told me, but I thought, no, you couldn't go that far, it would be unfair to give men exactly what they want. But she was lying on her back, the blanket leaving bare two white shoulders and her neck. I couldn't see clearly yet, so I ran my fingers from one shoulder, across her neck, to the other shoulder. Nothing blocked my finger's path—nothing, no straps, only taut, smooth skin. I still couldn't believe it, so I placed my index finger at the base of her throat and moved down, under the blanket, farther and farther down—one unbroken line—all the way. When I knew, I pulled my hand away. She moaned and turned away from me. I looked at my finger, placed it at the top of her spine and followed the hard bumps all the way down. I looked at my finger again, tasted it. Then I placed it against the back of her knee, under her nostrils, behind her ear, in the hair under her arm. And every place my finger touched, it pressed. And everywhere it pressed, her skin resisted with the same soft strength, and I thought, "This . . . is youth." I lay down and buried my nose against her scalp, my nose rubbing up and down as her foot rubbed against the sheets. When I woke up, it was just past dawn. The room was bright. That's when I tried to assault her—yes, it's true, I *tried*. But I'm an honorable man, so don't worry for her. If I had known she was a virgin, I would never have even thought of it to begin with.

(Pause.)

WOMAN: Well, this is too bad. You know the rules of the house, don't you?

KAWABATA: Yes.

WOMAN: But still . . .

KAWABATA: But I didn't.

WOMAN: Very technical.

KAWABATA: I don't know why. It was too bright in the room. I became sad, then angry. I wanted to hit her or something. But instead, I tried that instead.

WOMAN: Can I get you some tea?

KAWABATA: Huh? Yes, please. Thank you.

WOMAN: Why do you do that kind of thing anyway?

KAWABATA: I told you, I don't know. And don't make it sound like I do it often.

WOMAN: No, I mean about sleeping with your head in her hair.

KAWABATA: Oh, that.

WOMAN: Don't you worry about suffocating?

KAWABATA: I have my reasons.

WOMAN: Well, go on. There's very little you can't tell me now.

(Pause.)

KAWABATA: Her hair—the girl last night. It had a special smell. Like a lady friend of mine.

WOMAN: Your wife?

KAWABATA: No, I'm afraid not. Maybe thirty years ago. She was married to—oh, some kind of Hong Kong businessman, maybe even a movie producer—I can't remember. I do remember she lived alone with her servants—he was away—in a huge castle in Kowloon. It really was—a castle in Kowloon. I didn't know they had castles either. Where did we meet? Kyoto? I can't—you see, I'd even forgotten her until I smelled that girl's hair. My lady friend, I'd smell her hair and she'd cry, "Don't do that. It's filthy!" But I'd smell her hair for hours. I wonder what she's doing now. She was the only woman who ever winked at me.

WOMAN: Mr. Kawabata . . .

KAWABATA: I was shocked. This was many years ago, you know.

WOMAN: I apologize. For my hysteria.

KAWABATA: Have you . . . seen my point?

WOMAN: Yes.

KAWABATA: About the story? My writing?

WOMAN: Yes. Would you like to be our guest again tonight?

KAWABATA: What? Even after—?

WOMAN: I misjudged you. You are honest. That's a rare quality. I was irrational. This time, no charge. Only please stay.

KAWABATA: I came here to burn my record.

WOMAN: We can make you a new one. The girl I've picked out for you tonight is more experienced than the one before.

KAWABATA: It's not the same one?

WOMAN: No. Isn't it better to have a different one?

KAWABATA: You understand that I won't . . . do anything like . . . last night.

WOMAN: Of course, Mr. Kawabata. I see you're a gentleman after all. Your sleeping medicine?

KAWABATA: My—oh, thank you. I don't quite understand.

WOMAN: Don't understand. Just enjoy tonight's sleep. May I help you undress?

KAWABATA: Thank you. I suppose . . . I can't refuse your generosity.

WOMAN: Thank you.

(They go behind the screen. Again she helps him undress and put on a kimono.)

KAWABATA: Uh—where was your house located before?
WOMAN: Before? We've always been here.
KAWABATA: No, but that story you told—the one about your guest the policeman.
WOMAN: Oh, that.
KAWABATA: Where did you move from?
WOMAN: We didn't. *(Pause)* Things just worked out.

(They come out. She opens the door, gives him a key.)

Third door on your left. This one's even prettier—and more experienced.
KAWABATA: What do you mean, "more experienced"? After all, she's sound asleep.
WOMAN: Good night, Mr. Kawabata.

(He walks through the door; she closes it. She returns to the desk, pulls out her record book and begins to write. Lights to black.)

Scene Three

Evening, several months later. Kawabata is sitting alone. Silence. Woman enters from door to rooms.

WOMAN: Yes, I can arrange something tonight. *(Pause)* But you should know better. You've been a guest for five months now. Why didn't you call first, instead of just bursting in?
KAWABATA *(Sharply)*: I'm sorry!
WOMAN: It will be a few minutes before things are ready.

(Pause.)

KAWABATA: Can you give me some of that sleeping medicine?

WOMAN: Now? Well, if you like.

KAWABATA: No, not that. The kind you give the girls.

WOMAN: The girls?

KAWABATA: Yes. I want to sleep as deeply as they do.

WOMAN: Sir, that kind of medicine isn't healthy for old men.

KAWABATA: I can't take it. I'm your guest, aren't I? You always say so. You always say you want to serve your guests, don't you?

WOMAN: What's wrong with this? *(She holds up the usual cup)*

KAWABATA: I wake up. I wake up at two, three in the morning. Sometimes it takes me an hour to fall back to sleep. I just lie there.

WOMAN: Your body shouldn't be building up resistance.

KAWABATA: That's not it.

WOMAN: If you're tired of my girls, I can arrange something special.

KAWABATA: Will it help me sleep? *(Pause)* See? Whatever you do with the girls—it doesn't matter if I have to lie there like a stone.

WOMAN: Is there a girl here you'd like to see again?

KAWABATA: No. It's not the girls, it's me. When I began coming here, I'd lie awake at nights, too, but I'd love it, because I'd remember . . . things I'd forgotten for years—women, romances. I stopped writing—even exercises—it all seemed so pointless. But these last few weeks, I smell their skin, run my fingers between their toes—there's nothing there but skin and toes. I wake up in the middle of the night, and all I can remember was what it was like to remember, and I'm a prisoner in that bed.

WOMAN: I'm sorry. I can't—

KAWABATA: No. Listen. It's getting worse. Last night, when I woke up, all I could think of was the death of my friend.

WOMAN: I'm sorry.

KAWABATA: I hadn't thought of Mishima's suicide in a year. But last night—it began again—what must it have been like? *(Pause) Hara-kiri.* How does a man you know commit *hara-kiri?* A loved one, a friend. Strangers, of course. They kill themselves daily. But someone you know—how do they find that will? *(Pause)* The will. To feel your hands forcing steel through your stomach and if the hands stopped the pain would stop, but the hands keep going. They must become another being, your hands. Yes. Your hands become another being and the steel becomes you.

WOMAN: You shouldn't give your friend more respect than he deserves.

KAWABATA: He was a man, though. He had his lover stand behind him and chop off his head when the cutting was done.

WOMAN: I'm not going to give you dangerous drugs. I'm sorry. *(Pause)* Don't worry so much about your friend, Mr. Kawabata. People commit suicide for themselves. That's one thing I know. I had a sister, Mr. Kawabata. My parents sent her away to Tokyo, hoping that she would be trained in the tea, the dance, the *koto*, to attract a man of wealth. I wept with envy at the fine material Mother bought for her kimonos—gold thread, brocade. The day she left, I was angry—she was crying at her good fortune. Years went by; we were both engaged. She came back from Tokyo for her wedding and we could barely recognize her—she had neither the hands nor the speech of anyone we knew. I got very angry at her haughtiness. My chore was to pick the maggots from the rice, and I purposely left a few in, hoping she would get them . . . Their wedding was the most beautiful I'd ever seen. Just before she was to leave, my sister cornered me outside, tears streaming down her face, and begged my forgiveness . . . They tried to keep the story a secret from us, but, well . . . such a romantic story; the stuff legends are made of. It seems my sister had a lover in the village, that they had pledged fidelity long before she left for Tokyo. The

next morning, my father went to draw water from the
well. In the dim light before dawn, two faces came
rushing up to the water's surface. Two faces—my sister
and my fiancé . . . So don't worry about your friend, Mr.
Kawabata. People kill themselves to save themselves,
not others. *(Pause)* Now, I'm going to prepare something special. There will be two girls. There will be
twice the warmth.

*(She exits. He goes to the cabinet, takes out the vials and
a cup. He pours and drinks three glasses of the sleeping
potion. He returns the items. She reenters.)*

KAWABATA: Madame?

WOMAN: Yes.

KAWABATA: If I were to commit *hara-kiri*, would you chop
off my head?

WOMAN: Mr. Kawabata—

KAWABATA: No! Answer me. If I gave you a sword—I'd pay
you, you know—I wouldn't expect you to do it for
nothing.

WOMAN: This type of question doesn't help either of us.

KAWABATA: Listen—would you chop off my head when I
whispered, "Now. Please. Now." Or would you walk
away laughing, counting your change?

WOMAN: Will you stop that? Will you stop that selfishness?

KAWABATA: No! The question is—answer it!—would you
chop—

WOMAN: No! No! That's *your* question, yours only. You
never think of anyone else's suffering—you're so self-
centered, all you men, every last one of you. Have some
woman chop off your head, leave her alone, do you
think of her? She takes her few dollars, she buys some
vegetables, she eats and slowly withers away—no glory,
no honor, just a slow fading into the background—
that's all you expect. No, Mr. Kawabata, if *I* wanted to
commit *hara-kiri*, would you chop off *my* head?

KAWABATA: Women don't commit *hara-kiri*.

WOMAN: What if I did? What if I were the first?

KAWABATA: This is pointless.

WOMAN: I know—you think I would do it the woman's way, just slipping the tiny knife in here. (*Points to the base of her neck*) But what if I wanted to do it like a man? Completely. Powerfully.

KAWABATA: That's a foolish question.

WOMAN: I would do it better than you.

KAWABATA: Don't be absurd.

WOMAN: I would be braver.

KAWABATA: What a ridiculous notion!

WOMAN: If you didn't chop off my head, I'd be glad.

KAWABATA: This is a waste of time.

WOMAN: Because then, I'd be braver than you or your friend.

KAWABATA: Don't blaspheme Mishima.

WOMAN: I'd die like the generals.

KAWABATA: You're just an old woman.

WOMAN: I'd be the old woman who died like the generals.

KAWABATA: Show some respect.

(*Pause.*)

WOMAN: So quiet now, aren't you, Mr. Kawabata. Why don't you spout glorious phrases about chopping off my head? (*Pause*) Or why don't you write your report and destroy us all? (*Pause*) Your room is ready. Should I help you undress?

KAWABATA: No. (*He starts to leave, still dressed*)

WOMAN: Don't forget your key.

(*He returns, takes the key.*)

Fourth door on your right.

(*He exits. She closes the door. Pause. She goes to her desk, takes out a makeup kit. She stands next to the mirror, powders her face completely white, does her eyes, her mouth. She then goes to the door to the rooms, pulls up a chair and sits facing the door.*)

KAWABATA *(Offstage)*: Madame! Madame!

(He enters, wearing only his pants. He is in a panic, but the large amount of sleeping potion he's taken has started to take effect. He stares at her. She says nothing. He is speechless. Long pause.)

Your . . . one of your girls. She's . . . not breathing. No pulse.

WOMAN: Her body is being removed even as you speak. Now go back to bed. There is still the other girl.

KAWABATA: Other girl?

WOMAN: Yes, there were two, remember?

KAWABATA: I can't . . . your face. Why is it that way? I can't go back in there. She's dead. Do something. Go in.

WOMAN: Very little I can do. She took too much of her sleeping medicine, I think.

KAWABATA: This is inhuman.

WOMAN: It's difficult, but these things happen.

KAWABATA: This is . . . not human.

WOMAN: Now, go back. It won't do to be walking the streets at this hour.

KAWABATA: Why do people come here? Why don't they leave? I won't . . . I'm leaving.

WOMAN: You can't leave.

KAWABATA: I'm leaving. Where's my shirt, my coat?

WOMAN: Where will you go?

KAWABATA: Out. Home.

WOMAN: In your condition? Look at you—what happened, anyway?

KAWABATA: No, I don't care. I'll sleep in the streets.

WOMAN: You'll die in the cold, that's what you'll do.

KAWABATA: Yes. I'll die in the cold. I'll die in the cold before I become like Old Eguchi. Look at him—pathetic— here every damn night.

WOMAN: Like Old Eguchi? How are you *not* like Old Eguchi?

KAWABATA: I can still sleep somewhere else.

WOMAN: Today, perhaps. Tomorrow, no.

KAWABATA: Where's my shirt?

WOMAN: Here. *(She leads him to the mirror)* Look at yourself. Even as we speak, the lines are getting deeper, the hair is getting thinner, your lips are getting drier. Even as we speak, the shape of your face is changing, and with it, a mind, a will, as different as the face. You can leave now, Mr. Kawabata, but as much as you deny it, your face will continue to change, as if your will didn't even exist. See my face? Look at it. Close. I try and powder it like a young girl. But look—all that's here is an obscene mockery of youth. Don't be like this, Mr. Kawabata. Go back to sleep and let's not hear any more of your grandstanding.

(Kawabata is firmly in the grip of the drug now.)

KAWABATA: I'm . . . so tired. I drank too much of the potion.

WOMAN: That? I'm sorry. My fault. I shouldn't have left it there. Well, you should be all right. That's not as strong as the stuff you wanted.

KAWABATA: I would leave, I would, you know.

WOMAN: But you're too tired?

KAWABATA: I'm not coming back.

WOMAN: Of course not. Here. I'll help you to your room.

(She starts to sing the "Tokyo Ondo" softly as they exit together. As the lights fade slowly, we can still hear the song.)

Scene Four

A week later. It is evening. Kawabata is alone in the room. He is wrapping something in a small box. He completes the wrapping, puts the box into the breast pocket of the suit he is wearing. Woman enters from the door to the rooms. She carries a manuscript.

WOMAN: You've sent this to your publisher?

KAWABATA: Yes. It will be in print in time.

(Pause.)

WOMAN: You go very easy on yourself.

KAWABATA: In what sense?

WOMAN: You don't even name the main character after yourself. You call him Old Eguchi.

KAWABATA: Maybe I'm writing about him, not me.

WOMAN: And here . . . this story. That never happened. No man ever died here.

KAWABATA: Are you sure?

WOMAN: Who told you that?

KAWABATA: No one. I just thought . . . maybe.

WOMAN: And look at this. All this talk about the girls with their electric blankets. We don't even have electric blankets.

KAWABATA: Madame, I write stories, not newspaper copy. I don't—

WOMAN: This woman—she's very . . . uh . . . she seems so hard.

KAWABATA: The story's not about her.

WOMAN: She has no feelings, no heart. She's so . . . above it all, like she never cries, like her heart has gone through life without stumbling. She's like a ghost that walks through men's houses without creaking the floorboards.

KAWABATA: It's rather depersonalized, objective . . .

WOMAN: "Objective"? How can you say that? Look at the end—here—when the girl dies—like last week—and she says, "There's still the other girl." Doesn't that make her just one kind of woman?

KAWABATA: What I mean is that—

WOMAN: Doesn't it? Yes, I said that. But I shared things with you, stories. I let you see me ridiculous, hideous, a fool in my powder. Where is that? Is this all you remember? Just an old, cruel woman who serves you tea and takes your money?

KAWABATA: You have to understand . . . the joy was that I could finally write again at all.

WOMAN: Yes. That is surprising.

KAWABATA: I wasn't going to stop it.

WOMAN: I was surprised when we hadn't seen you all week.

KAWABATA: Do you understand?

WOMAN: Do you still think that the house will survive this story? Even after revealing the girl's death?

KAWABATA: I don't know. Who can say?

WOMAN: You didn't change anything, make it harder for them to find us.

KAWABATA: I'm sorry. I wanted to, but I couldn't. I'm sorry.

WOMAN: No. Sorry has nothing to do with it. We each do our work.

KAWABATA: When I told you last week—drugged—that I wasn't coming back again, did you believe me?

WOMAN: Of course not. But there was a part of me . . . *(Pause)* Up to a point, you'd acted like all my guests. The game with the tiles, being unable to assault my girl when you found her a virgin, you fit right into the gentleman's pattern. But your memories—leaving you so soon. There was a part of me that wondered. I wanted to call you. Once I even finished dialing your number. But I hung up before it rang. I sat here and thought up tortures for you. I thought you'd gone away . . . committed *hara-kiri*, and that you were waiting for me to come and chop off your head. I decided to stay right here.

KAWABATA: Did you think I wasn't coming back?

WOMAN: After a time, I began to wonder. *(Pause. She goes to the mirror, looks at it)* Well, there're many things I could do now. I could move to another city. Try to start again, from the ground. Or I could sit here, the same as always. Who knows? Perhaps no one will believe your story.

KAWABATA: That's quite possible. I've told you that.

WOMAN: Which would you recommend?

KAWABATA: Me? I don't know what kind of risks you take, or what's involved in starting over.

WOMAN: No. You don't.

KAWABATA: I think, though, that at our age, starting again is only worthwhile if one enjoys the process.

WOMAN: "At our age"?

KAWABATA: It's—uh—difficult to make long-range plans, you know.

WOMAN: Since when are we the same age?

KAWABATA: We are, aren't we?

WOMAN: Yes, we are.

KAWABATA: Give or take five years—

WOMAN: And you, then—

KAWABATA: —which hardly matters at this point.

WOMAN: —what will you do? Will you come back here?

KAWABATA: No.

WOMAN: Oh.

KAWABATA: No. My life becomes very simple now. *(He takes out a packet of bills, offers them to her)* Here. Here. Take it. Enough for you to . . . I don't know, buy a new house, anywhere you want. Or retire. Yes, retire and never worry about a thing again.

WOMAN: This is . . . so much . . . amazing. I can't take this. Why?

KAWABATA: I want you to serve me.

WOMAN: This is . . . an outrageous amount, Mr. Kawabata. I cannot accept it.

KAWABATA: Please. You'll need the money. An even trade.

WOMAN: Do you want a girl? A room?

KAWABATA: No.

WOMAN: I can fix you something special.

KAWABATA: Fix me some tea.

WOMAN: Oh, I forgot. I'm sorry.

KAWABATA: No. Don't apologize.

WOMAN: I'm sorry. So rude of me. It's such a cold night.

KAWABATA: You make very wonderful tea.

WOMAN: No, it's not.

KAWABATA: Yes.

WOMAN: It's nothing.

(Pause.)

KAWABATA: I've grown in this house.

WOMAN: You feel young here?

KAWABATA: I did. As I've slept here, I've grown older. I've seen my sweethearts, my wife, my mistresses, my daughters, until there's only one thing left.

(She comes with the tea.)

Will you powder your face again?

WOMAN: Mr. Kawabata, don't—

KAWABATA: Please.

WOMAN: You're mocking me—an old woman.

KAWABATA: No, I've brought you something. *(He reaches into a bag he is carrying, pulls out a kimono)*

WOMAN: Oh!

KAWABATA: Yes. Take it.

WOMAN: It's . . . No, this isn't for me.

KAWABATA: Yes. See? Gold thread. Brocade.

WOMAN: I can't accept this. Please. Give it to someone who deserves it.

KAWABATA: It's for you.

WOMAN: One of your young admirers. You are a famous writer. You must have many.

KAWABATA: Please. Put it on. It's just like the one you told me about.

WOMAN: It's gorgeous, too beautiful—

KAWABATA: Put it on and powder your face.

WOMAN: You're so foolish, Mr. Kawabata. I'll disgrace these clothes. Once they drape down my old bones, especially with my face in that powder, they'll change into something else completely, believe me.

KAWABATA: Don't be shy. You'll do me a great honor to wear my gift.

(Pause.)

WOMAN: If you insist.

KAWABATA: Yes. Please.

(She starts to leave.)

No. Please. Do it in here. I want to watch.

WOMAN: Women don't like men to watch them making up.

(Pause. She sits, begins making up.)

KAWABATA: I finished that story several days ago, you know. It came out of me like a wild animal, my hands were cramping at the pen. I wanted to show it to you while it was still warm, but I kept turning back. It's the same way I've felt before when I've written the end of a story, yet known that the story had more to do before I could rest. So I trusted my instincts—I watched television for two full days, since usually, what hasn't yet been revealed will rise to the surface in its own time. Yesterday, I woke up and knew what had to be added, and words weren't the question at all, so I sent the manuscript as it was to my publisher and went out shopping.

WOMAN: For the kimono? It's so beautiful.

KAWABATA: I tried to imagine the one you described.

WOMAN: This is every bit as beautiful.

KAWABATA: It's not the same?

WOMAN: It's difficult for me to remember. I was so young. But my sister's couldn't have been any finer.

(She takes the kimono, goes behind the screen, begins changing into it. He takes the small box out of his breast pocket, removes his jacket, takes off his tie, unbuttons his collar, takes off his shoes. Finally, she speaks:)

After the war, when we realized Father wasn't coming back, and the family was dispersed, I moved here to Tokyo. And I thought, "Now I'll dress in brocade also. I'll wear gold threads, too." But when I remembered my sister, I lost any desire to have anything like that. It's just as well, that being after the war and all. And I've never had the money, even to this day—ai! You'd think at my age, I'd have earned the right to stop worrying about money.

KAWABATA: But I've given you your security.

WOMAN: Yes, yes. I still can't—but why? *(She steps out from behind the screen)* See? Don't I look hideous?

KAWABATA: You're exactly what I want.

WOMAN: Is this what you want? An old hag pretending to be young again?

KAWABATA: Please. Sit down.

WOMAN: The tea—it's probably cold.

KAWABATA: No, it's fine. Open that box.

WOMAN: This one?

KAWABATA: Yes.

WOMAN: It's beautifully wrapped. *(She starts to open it)*

KAWABATA: It took me several hours to buy the kimono, and the rest of the day to buy that.

(She removes a vial of clear liquid.)

Please. Add it to the tea. *(Pause)* Go on. You said it was all right for us to bring our own medicine, didn't you? *(Pause)* The top lifts off. *(Pause)* Don't worry. I'm not going to ask you to drink it or anything. It's for me. Now, go on.

WOMAN: Respect me, Mr. Kawabata.

KAWABATA: I do.

WOMAN: Tell me—this isn't a sleeping potion.

KAWABATA: No.

WOMAN: Do you want a room?

KAWABATA: No.

WOMAN: I want to give you one. Free.

KAWABATA: I've already paid.

WOMAN: For what?

KAWABATA: Paid not to have a room.

WOMAN: For me?

KAWABATA: Please, empty the vial.

WOMAN: No.

(Pause.)

KAWABATA: Isn't this your job? Isn't this what you get paid to
do? For your life's security, madame, you should be
willing to endure a little more than usual. *(Pause)*
What's the matter? I thought of all people in the
world, you would understand this.

(Silence. She empties the vial into the teapot.)

Good. I'm sorry. I didn't mean to do that, say those things.
But I assume . . . we have an understanding. Do we?

WOMAN: Look at me. See this? *(Points to her face)* This?
(Pointing to her Kimono) That should answer your
question. What should I do now?

KAWABATA: Tell me again, why I should come to your house.

WOMAN *(As before)*: Our guests sleep very well here. It's the
warmth, they say.

KAWABATA: Warmth?

WOMAN: Our guests are not afraid to sleep at night. The
darkness does not threaten them.

KAWABATA: Oh, it's so cold tonight. Look at my hand. Could
you pour me some tea, please?

(Pause.)

WOMAN: Yes. Certainly.

*(She does; her eyes are fixed on him. She watches him
drink as she speaks.)*

The girl I've picked out for you is . . . she's . . . half
Japanese, half Caucasian, very beautiful, like a child,
like a pearly-white snowflake child, whose foot
never—always—moves, traces circles around the
snow—uh—sheet, fleeing—uh—feeling the warmth,
the heart—uh—the heat, finding it, the warmth, the
heart—uh—the heat, taking it, the warmth, the heat,
always . . .

(He puts down the cup. It's empty. She refills his cup. It sits on the table, untouched. Silence.)

KAWABATA: Now, we are as we should be.

WOMAN: Yes, I suppose so.

KAWABATA: And you look so beautiful.

WOMAN: Don't be cruel.

KAWABATA: But you do.

WOMAN: I won't listen.

KAWABATA: If we were thirty, maybe even twenty years younger, who knows?

WOMAN: Mr. Kawabata, for so long now, you've been trying to show me that you're different from my other guests.

KAWABATA: I'm sorry.

WOMAN: No, no, you've done it. You've gotten your wish. How does it make you feel?

KAWABATA: I wasted so much time.

WOMAN: You've proven to me that you're a thousand times more terrible and wonderful than any of my other guests.

KAWABATA: How sad. I don't even care about that anymore. If I'm different, it's only because I believed you when you showed me that I was the same as the rest of them. *(Pause)* It's funny. I've known you all this time, and I don't even know your name.

WOMAN: Michiko.

KAWABATA: Michiko. Wonderful. You have the hands of a young woman, did you know that, Michiko?

WOMAN: No. My hands are ugly.

KAWABATA: Let me see them, Michiko.

WOMAN: They are the hands of a crow.

KAWABATA: Please. Let me see them.

(She does.)

Amazing. And you—from the country. *(He touches them)* They are long. And firm. And warm with blood. *(He kisses them)* I'm starting to become tired. May I rest in your lap?

(She nods.)

Thank you, Michiko.

(Silently, she begins to stroke his hair.)

You've been very kind for allowing me to . . . take these liberties with you. I'm sorry I said those things about you. But I was afraid that you weren't as strong as I expected, that you couldn't give me what I needed. I shouldn't have doubted. *(Pause)* Please. Take the money. Be happy. Enjoy these last years. Buy what you've always wanted. *(Pause)* I do want you to take care of yourself. *(Silence)* You can't believe what a comfort it is for me to be falling asleep, yet able to open my eyes, look up, and see you.

(His eyes close. She looks around the house, continues to stroke his hair. She begins to sing the "Tokyo Ondo" as a lullaby. She picks up the remaining cup of tea, drinks it. She resumes singing and stroking his hair as lights fade to black.)

END OF PLAY

THE VOYAGE

(1992)

Libretto by

David Henry Hwang

for the Opera by Philip Glass

Production History

The Voyage was commissioned by the Metropolitan Opera in commemoration of the 500th anniversary of Columbus's arrival in America and opened October 12, 1992. It was conducted by Bruce Ferden; the production design was by David Pountney; the set design was by Robert Israel; the costume design was by Dunya Ramicova; the lighting design was by Gil Wechsler; and the choreography was by Quinny Sacks. The cast was as follows:

SCIENTIST/FIRST MATE	Douglas Perry
COMMANDER	Patricia Schuman
SHIP'S DOCTOR/SPACE TWIN 1	Kaaren Erickson
SECOND MATE/SPACE TWIN 2	Julien Robbins
ISABELLA	Tatiana Troyanos
COLUMBUS	Timothy Noble
EARTH TWIN 1	Jane Shaulis
EARTH TWIN 2	Jan Opalach

Characters

SCIENTIST/FIRST MATE, tenor
COMMANDER, soprano
SHIP'S DOCTOR/SPACE TWIN 1, soprano
SECOND MATE/SPACE TWIN 2, bass (lyric)
ISABELLA, mezzo
COLUMBUS, bass baritone
EARTH TWIN 1, mezzo
EARTH TWIN 2, bass
CHORUS, plays natives, the Spanish court at Granada,
    dignitaries and world rulers, dominican monks

Prologue

The opera begins with the Chorus, offstage, singing the Music of the Spheres. From the stars, the Scientist/First Mate, in wheelchair with computerized voice box, appears. During his aria, the Music of the Spheres can sometimes be seen to pose certain questions.

SCIENTIST/FIRST MATE:
 Quarks, kooks
 Heretics, lunatics
 Lovers and defilers of God
 Set off in leaky vessels
 Towards the holes on the horizon
 With faulty fuel lines
 And failing eyesight
 And limbs quite inadequate
 And minds finally limited
 To the certainty
 That the inadequate body can follow
 Where the inadequate mind has been

 When my daughter was born, I smiled like a hyena
 And for a moment I felt my legs and my limbs
 For a moment I knew
 No boundaries
 A body, a planet, a universe, a mind
 For whom the limits do not apply

 The voyage lies where
 The vision lies
 There

David Henry Hwang

CHORUS *(Simultaneously; repeated variously, fragmented)*:
    Will time run backwards?
    Is time a spherical object?
    Is real time imaginary?
    Can particles escape from a black hole?
    Does a finite universe exist without boundaries?
    Does God abhor a naked singularity?
    What is the mind of God?
    Can man picture a universe created without God?
    Does God have a purpose?

ACT I

Scene One

Commander, Scientist/First Mate, Ship's Doctor, Second Mate.
The interior of a spaceship as it hurdles out of control
toward our solar system. A time toward the end of our Ice
Age, about 50,000 B.C.

COMMANDER:
> No more choices
> Don't rely on options
> The concept of free will
> Is dead

SECOND MATE:
> My children are grandparents
> I should have studied law

SCIENTIST/FIRST MATE:
> Any fate is better
> Than another supper
> in the ship's mess hall

COMMANDER:
> Impulse power
> Damn the technicians
> The tradition of workmanship
> Is dead

SHIP'S DOCTOR:
> Think of my garden
> I plant in my garden, peas and carrots and lilies

COMMANDER:
> I did my training

In a box lined with buzzers
All hope of promotion
Is dead

SCIENTIST/FIRST MATE:

We're nearing a solar system.
Should I inquire?
Of course—look at her, she's preparing for death.

SECOND MATE:

Nothing could be worse than my wretched childhood.

SHIP'S DOCTOR:

And put out candles in case of a frost.

COMMANDER:

The lights do not flash
The eyes do not blink
The engines do not ignite
The beast rears its ugly head
And smiles, and licks its chops
And lies on the ground, tongue extended, to wait
For the dead

SCIENTIST/FIRST MATE:

An abundance of water
Twenty percent oxygen
Vegetation for CO_2
Humanoid forms
Shivering in their skins
Waiting
For the ice to melt

SECOND MATE:

Our horrible family outings

SHIP'S DOCTOR:

And, in the spring, oh, the children!

SECOND MATE:

Daddy, are we there yet?

SHIP'S DOCTOR:

Were there children?

SECOND MATE:

Are we there yet?

SHIP'S DOCTOR:
Were there children?
SECOND MATE:
Are we there yet?
SCIENTIST/FIRST MATE:
Commander, there is a planet
Where conditions are proper
COMMANDER:
For death?
SCIENTIST/FIRST MATE:
For life.
COMMANDER:
For life?
SCIENTIST/FIRST MATE:
Shall we go down?

(The spaceship crashes.)

Scene Two

The crew of the spaceship is now on the earth's surface.

SCIENTIST/FIRST MATE:
It appears to be a planet
In the infant stages of our own
COMMANDER:
The days of wandering
Are gone
No more floating
On the event horizon
Casually observing the death of a star
Now, we must keep our feet
Fixed to the soil
Pilot, may we have one last glimpse
Of the planet we are doomed to forget?
SCIENTIST/FIRST MATE:
As planets go, it was not so impressive

SHIP'S DOCTOR:
> It had an irregular orbit

SECOND MATE:
> The inhabitants played cards day and night

> *(As the Commander distributes the directional crystals,*
> *we hear a pulsating chord.)*

COMMANDER:
> Now each of us take
> One of the ship's directional crystals
> If a day arrives when we may return
> Any two brought together
> Will point the way home
> Pilot, will you set this crew
> Towards some less random destination?

SCIENTIST/FIRST MATE:
> Pilot yourselves
> Picture the world you would live in
> Then enter it
> This is the adventure
> Of life in the realm of gravity

> *(Musical interlude: The Commander distributes the glow-*
> *ing crystals among members of the crew. The Ship's*
> *Doctor and Second Mate close their eyes and begin mov-*
> *ing toward opposite sides of the stage. As they do, the*
> *pulsating chord begins to break up into its separate com-*
> *ponents, and the map of the galaxy fades away, replaced*
> *by images of the crew members' visions.)*

SECOND MATE:
> In my secret heart
> All I ever wanted
> Was to escape my home
> With no hope of return
> Now I see
> A world ruled by machines
> And my hand on the lever

As I look above
And I say, "There, the sky!
It is I who have turned it to black!"

(The Second Mate disappears into an image of Europe during the worst of the Industrial Revolution.)

SHIP'S DOCTOR:

In my secret heart
All I ever wanted
Was to tell my stories
To ears eager to hear
Now I see
A world gathered 'round
The tales from my mouth
Children and adults
Who listen for days and nights
As I begin: "Once upon a time"

(The Ship's Doctor disappears into an image of India, masses of people gathered around her.)

SCIENTIST/FIRST MATE:

In my secret heart
All I ever wanted
Was to continue the voyage
With vessel or without
Makes no difference to me

(The Scientist/First Mate is transported to a pavilion near the top of a Tibetan mountain.)

Scene Three

The Commander is left alone. She stares at the pulsating crystal in her hand.

COMMANDER:

In my secret heart

I would have rather died
Than live tethered to
The change of seasons
A ringing telephone
The endlessly repeating summer holiday
All I ever wanted
Was to kick up my heels
Without touching the ground
So I will simply walk
Into the arms of whatever lies waiting

(The Commander prepares to exit.)

What will they want from me?
Potions and jewels and color TV?
Or perhaps their hopes lie in the spiritual realm
A book of the dead, a mantra, some relics
Perhaps I will be enslaved
Carried aloft in the most shameful fashion
And will I come someday to mate?
With wordless grunts in a dark cave of groping?
Will I know what to do, where to touch, how to kiss?
Will I one day find myself loving the stranger?
Yes, I suppose that love and that hate
Mingle like blood between the sheets
When two worlds meet

(The perspective changes. Suddenly, we are with a large group of natives outside the spaceship. The Commander seems to them a fantastic creature, barely humanoid, speaking gibberish.)

NATIVES:
What will she want from us?
Potions and jewels and photos in color?
Or perhaps her hopes lie in the spiritual realm
A book of the dead, a mantra, some relics
Perhaps we will be enslaved
Carried aloft in the most shameful fashion

And will we come someday to mate?
With wordless grunts in a dark cave of groping?
Will we know what to do, where to touch, how to kiss?
Will we one day find ourselves loving the stranger?
Yes, I suppose that love and that hate
Mingle like blood between the sheets
When two worlds meet

(The commander is absorbed by the Natives, perform-ing the Rites of Spring.)

ACT II

Scene One

Columbus, Isabella, Scientist/First Mate, Second Mate, Chorus.
1492. The Spanish court at Granada. The Queen and
court bid Columbus bon voyage on his great expedition to the
Indies.

CHORUS:
    Admiral of the Ocean Sea
    Setting forth by our command
    Don Cristóbal Colón
    It is our will and pleasure
    That you be Admiral
    Viceroy
    Perpetual Governor-General
    Of all you shall win and discover
    And shall be empowered henceforth
    To call yourself
    Don Cristóbal Colón
    Your heirs and successors
    So entitled
    From rank to rank forever
    Amen

ISABELLA *(Interspersed with chorus)*:
    Qui navigant mare ennarent pericula eius
    Et audientes auribus nostris admirabimur
    Beati oculi qui vident quae vos videtis
    Et potestas a mari usque ad mare
    Et a fluminibus usque ad fines terrae

Et erunt reges nutritii tui
Et reginae nutrices tuae
[They that sail on the sea tell of the danger thereof
And when we hear it with our ears, we marvel thereat
Blessed are the eyes which see the things that ye see
And his dominion shall be from sea to sea
And from the river even to the ends of the earth
And kings shall be thy nursing fathers,
And their queens your nursing mothers]

CHORUS AND ISABELLA:
Amen

Scene Two

The "Amens" fade into the distance, as do Isabella and the court, literally. We find Columbus downstage, on board the Santa Maria. As his own "Amens" come to dominate the other voices, we realize we have been seeing a memory. In reality, he is far away on the sea, isolated, alone. It is October 11, 1492.

COLUMBUS:
Amen, amen

(Columbus's memories are violated by the Scientist/First Mate, calling out the dawn watch.)

Dawn of day thirty-two
And the memories of court
Their glorious voices
Have vanished beyond the horizon
Replaced
By infernal mumblings
Of men who pluck out
Their teeth with their fingers
And wipe their backsides
With the end of a rope

SCIENTIST/FIRST MATE:

    Bendita sea la luz
    Y la Santa Veracruz
    Y el Señor de la Verdad
    Y la Santa Trinidad
    Bendita sea el alma
    Y el Señor que nos la manda
    Bendito sea el día
    Y el Señor que nos lo envía
    [Blessed be the light of day
    And the Holy Cross we say
    And the Lord of Verity
    And the Holy Trinity
    Blessed be the immortal soul
    And the Lord who keeps it whole
    Blessed be the light of day
    And He who keeps the night away]

COLUMBUS:

    Yes, there are times
    When the faithful do waver
    And solitude takes us
    In its smothering arms
    And crushes, and crushes
    Our breath and our vision
    Until we lie gasping
    In madness and doubt

SECOND MATE:

    Oeste: nada del noroeste,
    Nada del sudoeste
    [West: nothing to the northward
    Nothing to the southward]

SCIENTIST/FIRST MATE:

    Leva el papahigo
    [Hoist the main course]

(Isabella appears upstage where the court had last been seen.)

ISABELLA:

>Empowered by God
>Your vision of such lucidity
>As if, in your hands,
>Lay already the kingdoms of Asia
>Such certainty, it is clear
>Can only have come from God
>Whose Word you disparage
>With all this weakness and weeping

SCIENTIST/FIRST MATE:

>Suban dos a los penoles
>[Two of you up on the yardarm]

COLUMBUS:

>But my vision has grown hazy
>As through the expanses of blue
>I see my own face, and it is old
>And it wonders

SECOND MATE:

>Tabla en buena hora,
>Quien no viniere que no coma
>[Table is set,
>Who don't come won't eat]

ISABELLA:

>The old men who wonder
>Are those who lacked faith while young
>Remember instead, the example of Noah
>Who faithfully awaited the coming birdsong

COLUMBUS:

>And in the hurlyburly of the waterworks
>Of random spouts and tidepools
>I seem to doubt even the order of God
>And the Turks and Jews we kill in His name

SECOND MATE:

>Oeste: nada del noroeste,
>Nada del sudoeste
>[West: nothing to the northward
>Nothing to the southward]

SCIENTIST/FIRST MATE:

¡Juegue el guimbalete para que la bomba achique!
[Work that pump brake till she sucks!]

ISABELLA:

Still your doubts, Don Cristóbal
Let my song smooth your salted brow
For the ocean is kind
The tides they are ordered
Each pass of the waves
Brings near to your feet
The evidence you seek

SECOND MATE:

¡Dad vuelta!
[Put your back into it!]

SCIENTIST/FIRST MATE:

Amén Dios nos de buenas noches
Buen viaje
[Amen and God give us a good night
And good sailing]

ISABELLA:

Don Cristóbal
It sometimes requires a woman
To rekindle the faith of a man

(Isabella is surrounded by a radiant holy light.)

Remember one, a child, a virgin
Who felt in her belly a stirring?
And held fast to the faith this was God?

COLUMBUS:

And do you promise me, oh blessed one,
Riches and governance,
And most of all,
That I further the kingdom of God?

*(Isabella steps downstage, toward Columbus, with every
step becoming more clearly a mortal woman.)*

ISABELLA:

Yes, I so swear
Now, you must as well
Will you hold to the faith
That Joseph took into the stable?

COLUMBUS:

You look to me
Like Dona Beatriz
Whose love I had sought in Gomera
Can it be? You come now as a woman
With flesh warmer than my own?

SCIENTIST/FIRST MATE AND SECOND MATE:

Salve Regina Mater
Misericordiae
Vita, Dulcedo et spes nostra salve
Ad Te clamamus exsules Filii Evae
[Hail, Holy Queen
Mother of Mercy,
Our life, our sweetness and our hope!
To thee do we cry, poor banished children of Eve]

ISABELLA:

I take many forms
I wear many faces
But all for the one righteous end
That the voyage you take
Is made in my name
And discoveries claimed for my honor
I am your Queen
I am your love
I am your one true God
Trust
Follow
Believe

SCIENTIST/FIRST MATE AND SECOND MATE:

Ad Te suspiramus Gementes et flentes
In hac lacrimarum valle eja ergo
Advocata nostra, illos tuos

Misericordes oculos ad nos converte
Et Jesum Benedictum fructum ventris tui
Nobis post hoc exilium ostende
O clemens, O pia
O Dulcis Virgo Maria
[To thee do we send up our sighs, mourning and weeping
In this valley of tears. Turn then,
Most gracious advocate,
Thine eyes of mercy towards us;
And after this our exile
Show us the blessed fruit of thy womb, Jesus.
Oh clement, oh loving,
Oh sweet Virgin Mary.]

*(The Scientist/First Mate and Second Mate embrace.
Offstage, a bird sings, indicating land is near.)*

SCIENTIST/FIRST MATE:
    ¡Lumbre! ¡Tierra!
    ¡Adelante! ¡Adelante!
    ¡Tierra! ¡Tierra!
    [Light my way! Land!]
    Onward! Onward!
    Land! Land!]

ACT III

Scene One

Space Twins 1 and 2, Earth Twins 1 and 2.
2092. The stage is split into two parts. One is a space sta-
tion in our solar system, commanded by Space Twins 1 and 2.
Behind them, a screen scans various sectors of the universe.
The other half is a research laboratory on earth, where Earth
Twins 1 and 2, both archeologists, meet carrying two of the
glowing crystals we saw in Act I. Each of the crystals emits a
particular sound frequency.

SPACE TWIN 1:
    All space exists
    In random disorder
SPACE TWIN 2:
    Be that as it may
    Our task is clear
    To order disorder
    By vectors and quadrants
    By infrared catalogs
    In the hope that one day
    A pattern will lead us
    To life
SPACE TWIN 1:
    Life?
    Sometimes I fear
    It is ghosts we seek
    In a black hole's pulsars
    Or a dwarf star's shadows

Could there somewhere
Really be beings
Who stare into space
And echo our foolish cry
"Yes, I will order disorder"

EARTH TWIN 1:
I was hiking in the Andes

EARTH TWIN 2:
I was digging near the Ganges

EARTH TWIN 1:
When I heard the most
Amazing sound
A tone high-pitched

EARTH TWIN 2:
Mine low

EARTH TWIN 1:
Unearthly

EARTH TWINS 1 AND 2:
As if the very rocks were
Lifting their voices
To heaven
How utterly coincidental

EARTH TWIN 1:
That the same event

EARTH TWIN 2:
Should befall us both

EARTH TWINS 1 AND 2:
On the very same day

(The Earth Twins bring their crystals together. As they do, the original pulsating chord is recreated. In the space station, the map onscreen rushes quickly through the universe until it indicates, as in Act I, the spot in the cosmos from whence came the original travelers.)

SPACE TWIN 1:
Sector 15, Vector 320,
Quadrant 1479

SPACE TWIN 2:
> Sound the alarms
> Radio the Chancellor
> Quick—alert the media!

> Six years in orbit
> Brought to its fruition
> I want a cold beer

SPACE TWIN 1:
> I want the Nobel Prize
> They'll give us six
> Three for you, three for me

> Quadrant 1479
> So far away

SPACE TWINS 1 AND 2:
> It will take us many, many years
> To reach such a destination

EARTH TWINS 1 AND 2:
> What a strange tone

EARTH TWIN 1:
> No radioactivity

EARTH TWIN 2:
> No stray particles

EARTH TWIN 1:
> Perhaps it is simply decorative

EARTH TWINS 1 AND 2:
> We'll run it through the standard battery

EARTH TWIN 1:
> But till then—

EARTH TWIN 2:
> It is—

EARTH TWINS 1 AND 2:
> Quite pleasantly hypnotical
> It will take us many, many years
> To reach our final conclusion

Scene Two

Commander, Space Twins, Scientist/First Mate.
    A spaceport. Several years later. An expedition is about to depart for the recently discovered planet, the source of life.

COMMANDER:
    Through the ages
    All we have sought to know
    What once had been believed unknowable

    Continuing this tradition
    We depart on our expedition
    Which will not reach its end
    Till the time of our children's children

    We cast off the earth
    And hereby ascend to heaven

    (A group of dignitaries and world rulers gathers to see off the explorers.)

DIGNITARIES AND WORLD RULERS:
    Secretary General of the United Nations
    Prime Minister of the EEC
    President of North America
    Chancellor of the United States of Africa
    Chairman of IT&T
    Controller of the South American Monetary Fund
    Executive Vice President of Coca-Cola
    Executive Director, World Environmental Council
    Emperor of China

    (The team of explorers heads into their spaceship. The door closes behind them as the acclaim of the chorus fades quickly away, replaced by the music of machines.)

Scene Three

*Inside the spaceship, each member of the expedition is alone
in his or her solitude; each wears a telephone headset through
which they say their good-byes.*

SCIENTIST/FIRST MATE:
  If you one day remarry
  Make sure that he loves children
COMMANDER:
  Be careful, my darling
  Your eyesight is poor at night
SPACE TWIN 2:
  Father, don't call me
  An undutiful child
SPACE TWIN 1:
  I loved the parade
  But now that it's over . . .
SCIENTIST/FIRST MATE:
  I always imagined
  A prom for my daughter
SPACE TWIN 2:
  I always imagined
  That you would be proud
COMMANDER:
  I always imagined
  This day might arise
SPACE TWIN 1:
  I always imagined
  A prize on my mantle
  But these obligations
  These stiff mock-heroics
  I never imagined
COMMANDER:
  I never imagined

That love would flow
Deeper than work

SPACE TWIN 2:

Then, hang up now
Good-bye

SCIENTIST/FIRST MATE:

I never imagined
The phone lines would end

SPACE TWIN 1:

Then life
Leads at last
To this solitude

SPACE TWIN 1:

The quest would devour
The very limits of my life

SCIENTIST/FIRST MATE:

Then love
Comes in three-minute increments

COMMANDER:

Then my heart
Had been braver than I had ever hoped

SCIENTIST/FIRST MATE:

Good-bye
To talks about nothing

SPACE TWIN 1:

To paper lanterns

SPACE TWIN 2:

Then, hang up now
Good-bye
Good-bye
So now it is clear
As earthbound illusions
And family myths
Fall like scales
From the eyes of St. Paul
That always
And ever

As I walked on my journey
I walked
As a child
With tiny feet
Walking alone

SPACE TWIN 1:
Good-bye
To prizes and politics

COMMANDER:
Good-bye
To the warm part of my heart

COMMANDER, SCIENTIST/FIRST MATE AND SPACE TWIN 1:
Good-bye
To the gem of my future
Good-bye
Good-bye
Hello
Hello

Epilogue

The space travelers fade away, revealing Columbus, lying on his deathbed. Dominican monks chant a requiem mass. The year is 1506. Isabella appears before Columbus.

COLUMBUS:
    They chant for me
    Am I to assume that I no longer live?
ISABELLA:
    Cristóbal Colón
    Cristóbal Colón
COLUMBUS:
    And now the song
    Of she who led me to sea
    But neglected even to call
    On her deathbed
    You promised me one-tenth of all I discovered
ISABELLA:
    Well, monarchs may change their minds
COLUMBUS:
    You promised me glory and honor
ISABELLA:
    I regret that you were brought back in chains
COLUMBUS:
    You promised that I would find Asia
    But cruelest of all
    You swore to me
    That I would magnify the kingdom of God
ISABELLA:
    I gave you next-best

David Henry Hwang

The Spanish Inquisition
Didn't you know my true face?
Didn't you see that your arrogant faith
Your blasted assurance
Was the child not of God
But of pride
The angel of vanity
Called by men, "Lucifer"?
And so, in His name,
You slaughtered the New World
And packed them away as slaves
In the hulls of your ships
Girls hung themselves
Bending their knees
As there was no room to stand
So, Cristóbal, come
Embrace me!
With this, your final breath
Come to my bed
Unzip me, defile me
Judge yourself, and enter my world

COLUMBUS:

Is it foolish to seek the mind of God
If there may be no God?
Is it futile to reach for order
In a universe built upon chaos?
Is it vanity to hope one day
To know the design of all things?
Even the sad expanses of regretful human souls?

From the first amoeba
Who fought to break free of itself
To Ulysses, to Ibn Battuta, to Marco Polo
To Einstein, and beyond
All that we seek to know
Is to know ourselves
To reduce the darkness

By some small degree
To light a candle, jump a stream
That the sum of human ignorance
Might dwindle just a bit
And the deeds done in darkness
May wither one day perhaps even
Expire

And if our human voyages
Are riddled sometimes with horrors
With pride, with vanity
With the mother's milk of cruelty
Yet finally human evil
Does not deny the good
Of knowledge
Of light
Of revelation
Of the hope that lo one day
Exploration will make obsolete
Even the sins of the explorer

ISABELLA:

Good-bye
Don Cristóbal
I see you resist my song

COLUMBUS:

I'm sorry I am unable to tarry here longer
But the journey that awaits
Is far more seductive than
All your last temptations
Finally
We take the voyage
When the voyage
Takes us

ISABELLA:

Good-bye
Don Cristóbal
Good-bye

COLUMBUS:
Finally
We take the voyage
When the voyage
Takes us

(Columbus's bed is transported to the stars.)

END OF OPERA

BONDAGE

(1992)

Production History

Bondage received its premiere at the Actors Theatre of Louisville (Jon Jory, Producing Director), as part of the 16th Annual Humana Festival of New American Plays, in Louisville, Kentucky, on March 1, 1992. It was directed by Oskar Eustis; the set design was by Paul Owen; the costume design was by Laura A. Patterson; the lighting design was by Mary Louise Geiger; the dramaturg was Deborah Frockt; and the stage manager was Debra Acquavella. The cast was as follows:

MARK	B. D. Wong
TERRI	Kathryn Layng

Characters

MARK
TERRI

Place

1990s.

An S&M parlor in the San Fernando Valley, California.

*A room in a bondage parlor. Terri, a dominatrix, paces with
her whip in hand in front of Mark, who is chained to the wall.
They both wear full face masks and hoods to disguise their
identities.*

MARK: What am I today?

TERRI: Today—you're a man. A Chinese man. But don't
bother with that accent crap. I find it demeaning.

MARK: A Chinese man. All right. And who are you?

TERRI: Me? I'm—I'm a blond woman. Can you remember
that?

MARK: I feel . . . very vulnerable.

TERRI: You should. I pick these roles for a reason, you know.
(She unchains him) We'll call you Wong. Mark Wong.
And me—I'm Tiffany Walker. *(Pause)* I've seen you
looking at me. From behind the windows of your—
engineering laboratory. Behind your—horn-rimmed
glasses. Why don't you come right out and try to pick
me up? Whisper something offensive into my ear. Or
aren't you man enough?

MARK: I've been trying to approach you. In my own fashion.

TERRI: How do you expect to get anywhere at that rate?
Don't you see the jocks, the football stars, the cowboys
who come 'round every day with their tongues hanging out? This is America, you know. If you don't assert
yourself, you'll end up at sixty-five worshipping a
Polaroid you happened to snap of me at a high school
picnic.

MARK: But—you're a blonde. I'm—Chinese. It's not so easy
to know whether it's OK for me to love you.

TERRI: C'mon, this is the 1990s! I'm no figment of the past. For a Chinese man to love a white woman—what could be wrong about that?

MARK: That's . . . great! You really feel that way? Then, let me just declare it to your face. I—

TERRI: Of course—

MARK: —love—

TERRI: It's not real likely I'm gonna love you.

(Pause.)

MARK: But . . . you said—

TERRI: I said I'm not a figment of the past. But I'm also not some crusading figure from the future. It's only 199—, you know. I'm a normal girl. With regular ideas. Regular for a blond, of course.

MARK: What's that supposed to mean?

TERRI: It means I'm not prejudiced—in principle. Of course I don't notice the color of a man's skin. Except—I can't help but notice. I've got eyes, don't I?

(Pause.)

I'm sure you're a very nice person . . . Mark. And I really appreciate your helping me study for the . . . physics midterm. But I'm just not—what can I say? I'm just not attracted to you.

MARK: Because I'm Chinese.

TERRI: Oh no, oh heavens, no. I would never be prejudiced against an Oriental. They have such . . . strong family structures . . . hardworking . . . they hit the books with real gusto . . . makes my mother green with envy. But, I guess . . . how excited can I get about a boy who fulfills my mother's fantasies? The reason most mothers admire boys like you is 'cause they didn't bother to marry someone like that themselves. No, I'm looking for a man more like my father—someone I can regret in later life.

MARK: So you're not attracted to me because I'm Chinese. Like I said before.

TERRI: Why are you Orientals so relentlessly logical?

(She backs Mark up around the room.)

MARK: Well, for your information . . . it doesn't—it doesn't hurt that you're not in love with me.

TERRI: Why not?

MARK: Because I never said that I loved you, either!

(They stop in their tracks.)

TERRI: You didn't?

MARK: Nope, nope, nope.

TERRI: That's bullshit. I was here, you know. I heard you open yourself up to ridicule and humiliation. I have a very good ear for that kind of thing. *(Cracks her whip)* So goddamn it—admit it—you said you love me!

MARK: I did not! If I don't tell the truth, you'll be angry with me.

TERRI: I'm already angry with you now for lying! Is this some nasty scheme to maneuver yourself into a no-win situation? God, you masochists make life confusing.

MARK: I came close. I said, "I love—" but then you cut me off.

TERRI: That's my prerogative. I'm the dominatrix.

MARK: I never finished the sentence. Maybe I was going to say, "I love . . . the smell of fresh-baked apple pie in the afternoon."

TERRI: That's a goddamn lie!

MARK: Can you prove it? You cut me off. In midsentence.

TERRI: It does . . . sound like something I would do. Damn. I'm always too eager to assert my superiority. It's one of the occupational hazards of my profession. *(Pause)* So I fucked up. I turned total victory into personal embarrassment. God, I'm having a rotten day.

MARK: Terri—

TERRI: Mistress Terri!

MARK: Mistress Terri, I—I didn't mean to upset you. It's OK. I wasn't really going to say I loved apple pie. Now—you can whip me for lying to you. How's that?

TERRI: I'm not about to start taking charity from my submissives, thank you. That's one good way to get laughed out of the profession. *(Pause)* Sorry, I just— need a moment. Wouldn't it be nice if they'd put coffeemakers in here?

MARK: Look—do what you want. I'm a Mexican man, and you're an Indonesian—whatever.

TERRI: What went wrong—was I just going through the motions?

(Mark places his hands gently on her shoulders.)

MARK: You feeling OK today?

TERRI: Of course I am! It just . . . hurts a girl's confidence to stumble like that when I was in my strongest position, with you at your weakest.

MARK: Why were you in such a strong position?

TERRI: Well, I was—a blond!

MARK: And why was I in such a weak one?

TERRI: Oh, c'mon—you were . . . an Oriental man. Easy target. It's the kind of role I choose when I feel like phoning in the performance. Shit! Now, look—I'm giving away trade secrets.

MARK: Asian. An Asian man.

TERRI: Sorry. I didn't know political correctness had suddenly arrived at S & M parlors.

MARK: It never hurts to practice good manners. You're saying I wasn't sexy?

TERRI: Well . . . I mean . . . a girl likes a little excitement sometimes.

MARK: OK, OK . . . look, let's just pretend . . . pretend that I did say, "I love you." You know, to get us over this hump.

TERRI: Now we're pretending something happened in a fantasy when it actually didn't? I think this is getting a little esoteric.

MARK: Terri, look at us! Everything we do is pretend! That's exactly the point! We play out these roles until one of us gets the upper hand!

TERRI: You mean, until *I* get the upper hand.

MARK: Well, in practice, that's how it's always—

TERRI: I like power.

MARK: So do I.

TERRI: You'll never win.

MARK: There's a first time for everything.

TERRI: You're the exception that proves the rule.

MARK: So prove it. C'mon! And—oh—try not to break down again in the middle of the fantasy.

TERRI: Fuck you!

MARK: It sort of—you know—breaks the mood?

TERRI: I'm sorry! I had a very bad morning. I've been working long hours—

MARK: Don't! Don't start talking about your life on my time!

TERRI: OK, you don't need to keep—

MARK: Sometimes, I really wonder why I have to be the one reminding you of the house rules at this late date.

TERRI: I didn't mean to, all right? These aren't the easiest relationships in the world, you know!

MARK: A man comes in, he plops down good money . . .

TERRI: I'm not in the mood to hear about your financial problems.

MARK: Nor I your personal ones! This is a fantasy palace, so goddamn it, start fantasizing!

TERRI: I have a good mind to take off my mask and show you who I really am.

MARK: You do that, and you know I'll never come here again.

TERRI: Ooooh—scary! What—do you imagine I might actually have some real feelings for you?

MARK: I don't imagine anything but what I pay you to make me imagine! Now, pick up that whip, start barking orders, and let's get back to investigating the burning social issues of our day!

TERRI (*Practically in tears*): You little maggot! You said you loved me . . . Mark Wong!

MARK: Maybe. Why aren't I sexy enough for you?

TERRI: I told you—a girl likes a little excitement.

MARK: Maybe I'm—someone completely different from who you imagine. Someone . . . with a touch of evil. Who doesn't study for exams.

TERRI: Oh—like you get "A"s regardless? 'Cause you're such a brain?

MARK: I have a terrible average in school. D-minus.

TERRI: I thought all you people were genetically programmed to score in the high nineties. What are you—a mutant?

MARK: I hang out with a very dangerous element. We smoke in spite of the surgeon general's warning. I own a cheap little motorcycle that I keep tuned in perfect condition. Why don't I take you up to the lake at midnight and show you some tricks with a switchblade? (*He plays with the handle of her whip*) Don't you find this all . . . a lot more interesting?

TERRI: I . . . I'm not sure.

MARK: I'm used to getting what I want.

TERRI: I mean . . . I wasn't planning on getting involved with someone this greasy.

MARK: I'm not greasy. I'm dangerous! And right now, I've got my eye set on you.

TERRI: You sound like some old movie from the '50s.

MARK: I'm classic. What's so bad about—?

TERRI: Oh, wait! I almost forgot! You're Chinese, aren't you?

MARK: Well, my name *is* Mark Wong, but—

TERRI: Oh, well . . . I'm certainly not going to go out with a member of the Chinese Mafia!

MARK: The Chinese—what? Wait!

TERRI: Of course! Those pathetic imitations of B-movie delinquents, that cheap Hong Kong swagger.

MARK: Did I say anything about the Chinese Mafia?

TERRI: You don't have to—you're Chinese, aren't you? What are you going to do now? Rape me? With your friends?

'Cause I've seen movies, and you Chinatown pipsqueaks never seem to be able to get a white woman of her own free will. And even when you take her by force, it still requires more than one of you to get the job done. Personally, I think it's all just an excuse to feel up your buddies.

MARK: Wait! Stop! Cut! I said I was vaguely bad—

TERRI: Yeah, corrupting the moral fiber of this nation with evil foreign influences—

MARK: Vaguely bad does not make me a hitman for the tong!

TERRI: Then what are you? A Vietcong? Mmmm—big improvement. I'm really gonna wanna sleep with you now!

MARK: No—that's even more evil!

TERRI: Imprison our hometown boys neck-high in leech-filled waters—

MARK: No, no! Less evil! Less—

TERRI: Will you make up your goddamn mind? Indecision in a sadomasochist is a sign of poor mental health.

MARK: I'm not a Chinese gangster, not a Vietcong . . .

TERRI: Then you're a nerd. Like I said—

MARK: No! I'm . . .

TERRI: . . . we're waiting . . .

MARK: I'm . . . I'm neither!

(Pause.)

TERRI: You know, buddy, I can't create a fantasy session solely out of negative images.

MARK: Isn't there something in between? Just delinquent enough to be sexy without also being responsible for the deaths of a few hundred thousand U.S. servicemen?

(Terri paces about, dragging her whip behind her.)

TERRI: Look, this is a nice American fantasy parlor. We deal in basic, mainstream images. You want something kinky, maybe you should try one of those specialty houses catering to wealthy European degenerates.

MARK: How about Bruce Lee? Would you find me sexy if I was Bruce Lee?

TERRI: You mean, like, "Hiiii-ya! I wuv you." *(Pause)* Any other ideas? Or do you admit no woman could love you, Mark Wong?

(Mark gets down on all fours.)

MARK: I'm defeated. I'm humiliated. I'm whipped to the bone.

TERRI: Well, don't complain you didn't get your money's worth. Perhaps now I'll mount you—little pony— you'd like that wouldn't you?

MARK: Wait! You haven't humiliated me completely.

TERRI: I'll be happy to finish the job—just open that zipper.

MARK: I still never said that I loved you, remember?

(Pause.)

TERRI: I think that's an incredibly technical objection this late in the game.

MARK: All's fair in love and bondage! I did you a favor—I ignored your mistake—well, now I'm taking back the loan.

TERRI: You are really asking for it, buddy . . .

MARK: After all, I'm not a masochist—no matter how this looks. Sure, I let you beat me, treat me as less than a man—

TERRI: When you're lucky . . .

MARK: But I do not say, "I love you"! Not without a fight! To say "I love you" is the ultimate humiliation. A woman like you looks on a declaration of love as an invitation to loot and pillage.

TERRI: I always pry those words from your lips sooner or later and you know it.

MARK: Not today—you won't today!

TERRI: Oh, look—he's putting up his widdle fight. Some- times I've asked myself, "Why is it so easy to get Mark to say he loves me? Could it be . . . because deep inside—he actually does?"

MARK: Love you? That's—slanderous!

TERRI: Just trying to make sense of your behavior.

MARK: Well, stop it! I refuse to be made sense of—by you or anyone else! Maybe . . . maybe you *wish* I was really in love with you, could that be it?

TERRI: Oh, eat me!

MARK: 'Cause the idea certainly never entered *my* head.

TERRI: Oh—even when you scream out your love for me?

MARK: That's what we call—a fantasy . . . Mistress.

TERRI: Yeah—*your* fantasy.

MARK: The point is, you haven't beaten me down. Not yet. You may even be surprised sometime to see that I've humiliated you. I'll reject *you* for loving me. And maybe, then, I'll mount *you*—pony.

TERRI *(Bursts out laughing)*: You can't dominate me. I'm a trained professional.

MARK: So? I've been your client more than a year now. Maybe I've picked up a trick or two.

TERRI: I'm at this six hours a day, six days a week. Your time is probably squandered in some less rewarding profession.

MARK: Maybe I've been practicing in my spare time.

TERRI: With your employees at some pathetic office? Tsst! They're paid to humiliate themselves before you. But me, I'm paid to humiliate you. And I still believe in the American work ethic. *(She cracks her whip)* So—enough talking everything to death! I may love power, but I haven't yet stooped to practicing psychiatry, thank you. OK, you're a—a white man and me—I'm a black woman!

MARK: African-American.

TERRI: Excuse me—are you telling me what I should call myself? Is this another of our rights you're dying to take away?

MARK: Not me. The Reverend Jesse Jackson—he thinks "African-American" is the proper—

TERRI: Who?

MARK: Jesse—I'm sorry, is this a joke?

TERRI: You're not laughing, so I guess it's not. Tell me—the way you talk . . . could you be . . . a liberal?

MARK: Uh, yes, if you speak in categories, but—

TERRI: Um. Well, then that explains it.

MARK: Explains what?

TERRI: Why I notice you eyeing me up every time I wander towards the bar.

MARK: Let me be frank. I . . . saw you standing here, and thought to myself, That looks like a very intelligent woman.

(Terri laughs.)

Sorry. Did I—say something?

TERRI: What do they do? Issue you boys a handbook?

MARK: What?

TERRI: You know, for all you white liberals who do your hunting a little off the beaten track?

MARK: Now, look here—

TERRI: 'Cause you've all got the same line. You always start talking about our "minds," then give us this *look* like we're supposed to be grateful—"Aren't you surprised?" "Ain't I sensitive?" "Wouldn't you like to oil up your body and dance naked to James Brown?"

MARK: I can't believe . . . you're accusing *me* of—

TERRI: Then again, what else should I have expected at a PLO fundraiser? So many white liberals, a girl can't leave the room without one or two sticking to her backside.

MARK: Listen—all I said was I find you attractive. If you can't deal with that, then maybe . . . maybe *you're* the one who's prejudiced.

TERRI: White people—whenever they don't get what they want, they always start screaming "reverse racism."

MARK: Would you be so . . . derisive if I was a black man?

TERRI: You mean, an African-American?

MARK: Your African-American brothers aren't afraid to date white women, are they? No, in fact, I hear they treat them better than they do their own sisters, doesn't that bother you even a bit?

TERRI: And what makes you such an expert on black men? Read a book by some other whitey?

MARK: Hey—I saw *Jungle Fever*.

TERRI: For your urban anthropology class?

MARK: Don't get off the subject. Of you and me. And the dilemma I know you're facing. Your own men, they take you for granted, don't they? I think you should be a little more open-minded, unless you wanna end up like the forty percent of black women over thirty who're never even gonna get married in their lifetimes.

(Silence.)

TERRI: Who the fuck do you think you are? Trying to intimidate me into holding your pasty white hand? Trying to drive a wedge through our community?

MARK: No, I'm just saying, look at the plain, basic—

TERRI: You say you're attracted to my intelligence? I saw you checking out a lot more than my eyes.

MARK: Well, you do seem . . . sensuous.

TERRI: Ah. Sensuous. I can respect a man who tells the truth.

MARK: That's a . . . very tight outfit you've got on.

TERRI: Slinky, perhaps?

MARK: And when you talk to me, your lips . . .

TERRI: They're full and round—without the aid of collagen.

MARK: And—the way you walked across the room . . .

TERRI: Like a panther? Sleek and sassy. Prowling—

MARK: Through the wild.

TERRI: Don't you mean, the jungle?

MARK: Yes, the . . . Wait, no! I see where you're going!

TERRI: Big deal, I was sniffing your tracks ten miles back. I'm so wild, right? The hot sun blazing. Drums beating in the distance. Pounding, pounding . . .

MARK: That's not fair—!

TERRI: Pounding that Zulu beat.

MARK: You're putting words into my mouth . . .

TERRI: No, I'm just pulling them out, liberal.

(Terri cracks her whip, driving Mark away from her.)

What good is that handbook now? Did you forget? Forget you're only supposed to talk about my mind? Forget that a liberal must never ever reveal what's really on his?

MARK: I'm sorry. I'm sorry . . . Mistress!

TERRI: On your knees, liberal!

(Terri runs the heel of her boot over the length of Mark's body.)

You wanted to have a little fun, didn't you? With a wild dark woman whose passions drown out all her inhibitions.

(Terri pushes Mark onto his back, puts the heel of her shoe to his lips.)

I'll give you passion. Here's your passion.

MARK: I didn't mean to offend you.

TERRI: No, you just couldn't help it. C'mon—suck it. Like the lily-white baby boy you are.

(Mark fellates on her heel.)

That statistic about black women never getting married? What'd you do—study up for today's session? You thought you could get the best of me—admit it, naughty man, or I'll have to spank your little butt purple.

MARK: I didn't study—honest!

TERRI: You hold to that story? Then Mama has no choice but to give you what you want— roll over!

(Mark rolls onto his stomach.)

You actually thought you could get ahead of me on current events!

(Terri whips Mark's rear during the next few lines.)

MARK: No, I mean—that statistic—it was just—

TERRI: Just *what?*

MARK: Just street knowledge!

TERRI: Street knowledge? Where do you hang out—the Census Bureau? Liar!

(Terri pokes at Mark's body with the butt of her whip.)

Don't you know you'll never defeat me? This is your game—to play all the races—but me—I've already become all races. You came to the wrong place, sucker. Inside this costume live the intimate experiences of ethnic groups that haven't even been born. *(Pause)* Get up. I'm left sickened by that little attempt to assert your will. We'll have to come up with something really good for such an infraction.

MARK: Can I—can I become Chinese again?

TERRI: What is your problem? It's not our practice to take requests from the customers.

MARK: I—don't want you to make things easy on me. I want to go back to what you call a position of weakness. I want you to pull the ropes tight!

TERRI *(Laughs):* It's a terrible problem with masochists, really. You don't know whether being cruel is actually the ultimate kindness. You wanna be the lowest of the low? Then beg for it.

(Mark remains in a supplicant position for the following ritual as Terri casually tidies the room.)

MARK: I desire to be the lowest of men.

TERRI: Why?

MARK: Because my existence is an embarrassment to all women.

TERRI: And why is that?

MARK: Because my mind is dirty, filled with hateful thoughts against them. Threats my weakling body can never make good on—but I give away my intentions at every turn—my lustful gaze can't help but give offense.

TERRI: Is that why you desire punishment?

MARK: Yes. I desire punishment.

TERRI: But you'll never dominate your mistress, will you? *(Pause)* Will you?! *(She cracks her whip)* All right. Have it your way. I think there's an idea brewing in that tiny brain of yours. You saw me stumble earlier tonight—then, you felt a thrill of exhilaration—however short-lived—with your forty-percent statistic. All of a sudden, your hopes are raised, aren't they? God, it pisses me off more than anything to see hope in a man's eyes. It's always the final step before rape. *(Pause)* It's time to nip hope in the bud. You'll be your Chinese man, and me—I'll be an Asian woman, too. *(Pause)* Have you been staring at me across the office—Mark Wong?

MARK: Who? Me?

TERRI: I don't see anyone else in the room.

MARK: I have to admit—

TERRI: What?

MARK: You are . . . very attractive.

TERRI: It's good to admit these things. Don't you feel a lot better already? You've been staring at me, haven't you?

MARK: Maybe . . .

TERRI: No, you don't mean "maybe."

MARK: My eyes can't help but notice . . .

TERRI: You mean, "Yes, sir, that's my baby." The only other Asian-American in this office.

MARK: It does seem like we might have something in common.

TERRI: Like what?

MARK: Like—where'd your parents come from?

TERRI: Mom's from Chicago, Dad's from Stockton.

MARK: Oh.

TERRI: You didn't expect me to say "Hong Kong" or "Hiroshima," did you?

MARK: No, I mean—

TERRI: Because that would be a stereotype. Why—are *you* a foreigner?

MARK: No.

TERRI: I didn't necessarily think so—

MARK: I was born right here in Los Angeles!

TERRI: But when you ask a question like that, I'm not sure.

MARK: Queen of Angels Hospital!

TERRI: Mmmm. What else do you imagine we might have in common?

MARK: Well, do you ever . . . feel like people are pigeonholing you? Like they assume things?

TERRI: What kinds of things?

MARK: Like you're probably a whiz at math and science? Or else a Vietcong?

TERRI: No! I was editor of the paper in high school, and the literary journal in college.

MARK: Look, maybe we're getting off on the wrong foot here.

TERRI: Actually, there *is* one group of people that does categorize me, now that you mention it.

MARK: So you *do* understand.

TERRI: Asian men. *(Pause)* Asian men who just assume because we shared space in a genetic pond millions of years ago that I'm suddenly their property when I walk into a room. Or an office. *(Pause)* Now get this straight. I'm not interested in you, OK? In fact, I'm generally not attracted to Asian men. I don't have anything against them personally, I just don't date them as a species.

MARK: Don't you think that's a little prejudiced? That you're not interested in me because of my race? And it's even your own? I met this black girl a few minutes ago—she seemed to support *her* brothers.

TERRI: Well, her brothers are probably a lot cuter than mine. Look, it's a free country. Why don't you do the same? Date a Caucasian woman.

MARK: I tried that too . . . a couple of women back.

TERRI: I'll tell you why you don't. Because you Asian men are all alike—you're looking for someone who reminds you of your mothers. Who'll smile at the lousiest jokes and spoon rice into your bowl while you just sit and grunt. Well, I'm not about to date any man who reminds me even slightly of my father.

MARK: But a blond rejected me because I *didn't* remind her of her father.

TERRI: Of course you didn't! You're Asian!

MARK: And now, you won't date me because I *do* remind you of yours?

TERRI: Of course you do! You're Asian!

(Pause.)

MARK: How—how can I win here?

TERRI: It's simple. You can't. Have you ever heard of historical karma? That's the notion that cultures have pasts that eventually catch up with them. For instance, white Americans were evil enough to bring Africans here in chains—now, they should pay for that legacy. Similarly, Asian men have oppressed their women for centuries. Now, they're paying for their crime by being passed over for dates in favor of white men. It's a beautiful way to look at history, when you think about it.

MARK: Why should my love life suffer for crimes I didn't even commit? I'm an American!

TERRI: C'mon—you don't expect me to buck the wheel of destiny, do you? This is the 1990s—every successful Asian woman walks in on the arm of a white man.

MARK: But—but what about Italian men? Or Latinos? Do you like them?

TERRI: I find them attractive enough, yes.

MARK: Well, what about their cultures? Aren't they sexist?

TERRI: Why do you stereotype people like that? If pressed, I would characterize them as macho.

MARK: Macho? And Asian men aren't?

TERRI: No—you're just sexist.

MARK: What's the difference?

TERRI: The—I dunno. Macho is . . . sexier, that's all. You've never been known as the most assertive of men.

MARK: How can we be not assertive enough and too oppressive all at the same time?

TERRI: It's one of the miracles of your psychology. Is it any
wonder no one wants to date you?

MARK: Aaargh! You can't reject me on such faulty reasoning!

TERRI: I can reject you for any reason I want. That's one of
the things which makes courtship so exciting. *(Pause)*
It seems obvious now, the way you feel about me,
doesn't it?

MARK: It does not!

TERRI: C'mon—whether black, blond or Asian—I think
the answer is the same. You . . . what?

MARK: I . . . find you attractive . . .

TERRI: Give it up! You feel something—something that's
driving you crazy.

MARK: All right! You win! I love you!

TERRI: Really? You do? Why, young man—I had no idea!
(Pause) I'm sorry . . . but I could never return your
affections, you being so very unlovable and all. In fact,
your feelings offend me. And so I have no choice but to
punish you.

MARK: I understand. You win again. *(He heads for the
shackles on the wall)*

TERRI: Say it again. Like you mean it.

MARK: You win! I admit it!

TERRI: Not that—the other part!

MARK: You mean, "I love you"? Mistress Terri, I love you.

TERRI: No! More believable! The last thing anyone wants is
an apathetic slave!

MARK: But I *do* love you! More than any woman—

TERRI: Or man?

MARK: Or anything—any creature—any impulse . . . in my
own body—more than any part of my body . . . that's
how much I love you.

(Pause.)

TERRI: You're still not doing it right, damn it!

MARK: I'm screaming it like I always do—I was almost getting poetic there . . .

TERRI: Shut up! It's just not good enough. *You're* not good enough. I won't be left unsatisfied. Come here.

MARK: But—

TERRI: You wanna know a secret? It doesn't matter what you say—there's one thing that always makes your words ring false—one thing that lets me know you're itching to oppress me.

MARK: Wha—what do you mean?

TERRI: I don't think you want to hear it. But maybe . . . maybe I want to tell you anyway.

MARK: Tell me! I can take the punishment.

TERRI: What sickens me most . . . is that you feel compelled to play these kinds of parlor games with me.

MARK: What—what the hell are you—?!

TERRI: I mean, how can you even talk about love? When you can't approach me like a normal human being? When you have to hide behind masks and take on these ridiculous roles?

MARK: You're patronizing me! Don't! Get those ropes on me!

TERRI: Patronizing? No, I've *been* patronizing you. Today, I can't even keep up the charade! I mean, your entire approach here—it lets me know—

MARK: I don't have to stand for this!

TERRI: That you're afraid of any woman unless you're sure you've got her under control!

MARK: This is totally against all the rules of the house!

TERRI: Rules, schmules! The rules say I'm supposed to grind you under my heel! They leave the details to me—sadism is an art, not a science. So—beg for more! Beg me to tell you about yourself!

(Panicked, Mark heads for the wall and tries to shackle himself.)

MARK: No! If I'm—if I'm defeated, I must accept my punishment fair and square.

TERRI: You're square all right. Get your arms out of there! Stand like a man! Beg me to tell you who you are.

MARK: If I obey, will you reward me by denying my request?

TERRI: Who knows? Out of generosity, I might suddenly decide to grant it.

MARK: If you're determined to tell me either way, why should I bother to beg?

TERRI: For your own enjoyment.

MARK: I refuse! You've never done something like this before!

TERRI: That's why I'm so good at my job. I don't allow cruelty to drift into routine. Now, beg!

MARK: Please, Mistress Terri . . . will you . . . will you tell me who I really am?

TERRI: You want to know—you wanna know bad, don't you?

MARK: No!

TERRI: In the language of sadomasochism, "no" almost always means "yes."

MARK: No, no, no!

TERRI: You are an eager one, aren't you?

MARK: I just don't like you making assumptions about me! Do you think I'm some kind of emotional weakling, coming in here because I can't face the real world of women?

TERRI: That would be a fairly good description of all our clients.

MARK: Maybe I'm a lot more clever than you think! Do you ever go out there? Do you know the opportunities for pain and humiliation that lurk outside these walls?

TERRI: Well, I . . . I *do* buy groceries, you know.

MARK: The rules out there are set up so we're all bound to lose.

TERRI: And the rules in here are so much better?

MARK: The rules here . . . protect me from harm. Out there—I walk around with my face exposed. In here, when I'm rejected, beaten down, humiliated—it's not me. I have no identifying features, and so . . . I'm no longer human. *(Pause)* And that's why I'm not pathetic to come here. Because someday, I'm going to beat you. And on that day, my skin will have become so thick, I'll be impenetrable to harm. I won't need a mask to keep my face hidden. I'll have lost myself in the armor. *(He places his wrists into the wall shackles)* OK—I bent to your will. You defeated me again. So strap me up. Punish me.

TERRI: But why . . . why all these fantasies about race?

MARK: Please, enough!

TERRI: I mean, what race *are* you, anyway?

MARK: You know, maybe we should just talk about *your* real life, how would you like that?

(Pause.)

TERRI: Is that what you want?

MARK: No . . .

TERRI: Is that a "no" no, or a "yes" no?

MARK: Yes. No. Goddamn it, I paid for my punishment, just give it to me!

(Terri tosses away her whip, begins to strap him up.)

What are you doing?

TERRI: Punishment is, by definition, something the victim does not appreciate. The fact that you express such a strong preference for the whip practically compels me not to use it. *(Pause)* I think I'd prefer . . . to kill you with kindness.

(Terri begins kissing the length of Mark's body.)

MARK: Please! This isn't . . . what I want!

TERRI: Are you certain? Maybe . . . I feel something for you. After all, you've made me so very angry. Maybe . . . you're a white man, I'm a white woman—there's nothing mysterious—no racial considerations whatsoever.

MARK: That's . . . too easy! There's no reason you wouldn't love me under those conditions.

TERRI: Are you crazy? I can think of a couple dozen off the top of my head. You don't have to be an ethnic minority to have a sucky love life.

MARK: But there's no . . . natural barrier between us!

TERRI: Baby, you haven't dated many white women as a white man lately. I think it's time to change all that. *(Pause; she steps away)* So—Mark . . . Walker. Mark Walker—how long has it been? Since anyone's given you a rubdown like that?

(Pause.)

MARK: I usually . . . avoid these kinds of situations . . .

TERRI: Why are you so afraid?

MARK: My fright is reasonable. Given the conditions out there.

TERRI: What conditions? Do you have, for instance, problems with . . . interracial love?

MARK: Whatever gave you that idea?

TERRI: Well, you . . . remind me of a man I see sometimes . . . who belongs to all races . . . and none at all. I've never met anyone like him before.

MARK: I'm a white man! Why wouldn't I have problems? The world is changing so fast around me—you can't even tell whose country it is anymore. I can't hardly open my mouth without wondering if I'm offending, if I'm secretly revealing to everyone but myself . . . some hatred, some hidden desire to strike back . . . breeding within my body. *(Pause)* If only there were some certainty—whatever it might be—OK, let the feminists rule the place! We'll call it the United States of Amazonia! Or the Japanese! Or the gays! If I could only figure out who's in charge, then I'd know where I stand. But this constant flux—who can endure it? I'd rather crawl into a protected room where I know what to expect—painful though that place may be. *(Pause)* I mean . . . we're heading towards the millennium. Last time, people ran fearing the end of the world.

They hid their bodies from the storms that would inevitably follow. Casual gestures were taken as signs of betrayal and accusation. Most sensed that the righteous would somehow be separated from the wicked. But no one knew on which side of such a division they themselves might fall.

(Silence.)

TERRI: You want to hear about yourself. You've been begging for it so long—in so many ways.

MARK: How do you know I just said anything truthful? What makes you so sure I'm really a white man?

TERRI: Oh, I'm not. After all these months, I wouldn't even care to guess. When you say you're Egyptian, Italian, Spanish, Mayan—you seem to be the real thing. So what if we just say . . . *(Pause; she releases him from the shackles)* You're a man, and you're frightened, and you've been ill-used in love. You've come to doubt any trace of your own judgment. You cling to the hope that power over a woman will blunt her ability to harm you, while all the time you're tormented by the growing fear that your hunger will never be satisfied with the milk of cruelty. *(Pause)* I know. I've been in your place.

MARK: You . . . you've been a man? What are you saying?

TERRI: You tell me. Fight back. Tell me about me. And make me love every second of it.

MARK: All right. Yes.

TERRI: Yes . . . WHO?

MARK: Yes, Mistress Terri!

TERRI: Yes—who?

MARK: Yes . . . whoever you are . . . a woman who's tried hard to hate men for what they've done to her but who . . . can't quite convince herself.

(Terri pushes Mark to the ground.)

TERRI: Is that what you think? *(Beat)* Tell me more . . .

MARK: You went out—into the world . . . I dunno, after college maybe—I think you went to college . . .

TERRI: Doesn't matter.

MARK: But the world—it didn't turn out the way you planned . . . rejection hung in the air all around you—in the workplace, in movies, in the casual joking of the population. The painful struggle . . . to be accepted as a spirit among others . . . only to find yourself constantly weighed and measured by those outward bits of yourself so easily grasped, too easily understood. Maybe you were harassed at work—maybe even raped—I don't know.

TERRI: It doesn't matter. The specifics never matter.

MARK: So you found your way here—somehow—back of the *Hollywood Star*—something—roomfuls of men begging to be punished for the way they act out there—wanting you to even the score—and you decided—that this was a world you could call your own.

TERRI: And so, I learned what it feels like to be a man. To labor breathlessly accumulating power while all the time it's dawning how tiring, what a burden, how utterly numbing—it is actually to possess. The touch of power is cold like metal. It chafes the skin, but you know nothing better to hold to your breast. So you travel down this blind road of hunger—constantly victimizing yourself in the person of others—until you despair of ever again feeling warm or safe—until you forget such possibilities exist. Until they become sentimental relics of a weaker man's delusions. And driven by your need, you slowly destroy yourself. *(She starts to remove her gloves)* Unless, one day, you choose to try something completely different.

MARK: What are you doing? Wait!

TERRI: It's a new game, Mark. A new ethnic game. The kind you like.

MARK: We can't play—without costumes.

TERRI: Oh, but it's the wildest interracial fantasy of all. It's called . . . two hearts meeting in a bondage parlor on

the outskirts of Encino. With skins—more alike than
not. *(She tosses her gloves away)* Haven't we met
before? I'm certain we have. You were the one who
came into my chamber wanting to play all the races.

MARK: Why are you doing this to me? I'm the customer here!

TERRI: No, your time is up. Or haven't you kept your eyes on
the clock? At least I know I'm not leaving you bored.

MARK: Then . . . shouldn't I be going?

TERRI: If you like. But I'm certain we've met before. I found
it so interesting, so different, your fantasy. And I've always
been a good student, a diligent employee. My daddy
raised me to take pride in all of America's service profes-
sions. So I started to . . . try and understand all the races I
never thought of as my own. Then, what happened?

MARK: You're asking me?

TERRI: C'mon—let me start you off. I have a box in my
closet—

*(Terri runs her bare hands up and down Mark's body as
he speaks:)*

MARK: In which you keep all the research you've done . . .
for me. Every clipping, magazine article, ethnic jour-
nals, transcripts from *Phil Donahue*. Blacks against
Jews in Crown Heights—your eyes went straight to the
headlines. The rise of neo-Nazism in Marseilles and
Orange County. And then, further—the mass-murder-
er in Canada who said, "The feminists made me do it."
You became a collector of all the rejection and rage in
this world. *(Pause)* Am I on the right track?

TERRI: Is that what you've been doing?

MARK: And that box—that box is overflowing now. Books are
piled high to the hems of your dresses, clippings slide out
from beneath the door. And you . . . you looked at it . . .
maybe this morning . . . and you realized your box was . . .
full. And so you began to stumble. You started to feel
there was nothing more here for you.

TERRI: If you say it, it must be true.

MARK: Is it?

(Terri starts to unlace her thigh-high boots.)

TERRI: I'm prepared to turn in my uniform and start again from here.

MARK: You're quitting your job?

TERRI: The masks don't work. The leather is pointless. I'm giving notice as we speak.

MARK: But—what if I'm wrong?

TERRI: I'm afraid I'll have to take that chance.

MARK: No, you can't just—what about your hatred of men? Are you really going to just throw it all away when it's served you so well?

TERRI: I've been a man. I've been a woman. I've been color- ful and colorless. And now, I'm tired of hating myself.

(Pause.)

MARK: And what about me?

TERRI: That's something you'll have to decide.

MARK: I'm not sure I can leave you. Not after all this time.

TERRI: Then stay. And strip. As lovers often do.

(As Terri removes her costume, Mark turns and looks away.)

MARK: I worry when I think about the coming millennium. Because it feels like all labels have to be rewritten, all assumptions reexamined, all associations redefined. The rules that governed behavior in the last era are crumbling, but those of the time to come have yet to be written. And there is a struggle brewing over the shape of these changing words, a struggle that begins here, now, in our hearts, in our shuttered rooms, in the light- ning decisions that appear from nowhere.

(Terri has stripped off her costume, except for her hood. She wears a simple bra and panties. Mark turns to look at her.)

I think you're very beautiful.

TERRI: Even without the metal and leather?

MARK: You look . . . soft and warm and gentle to the touch.

TERRI: I'm about to remove my hood. I'm giving you fair warning.

MARK: There's . . . only one thing I never managed to achieve here. I never managed to defeat you.

TERRI: You understand me. Shouldn't I be a lot more frightened? But—the customer is always right. So come over here. This is my final command to you.

MARK: Yes, Mistress Terri.

TERRI: Take off my hood. You want to—admit it.

MARK: Yes. I want to.

TERRI: The moment you remove this hood, I'll be completely exposed, while you remain fully covered. And you'll have your victory by the rules of our engagement, while I—I'll fly off over the combat zone.

(Terri places Mark's left hand on her hood.)

So congratulations. And good-bye.

(With his right hand, Mark undoes his own hood instead. He takes it off. He is an Asian man.)

You disobeyed me.

MARK: I love you.

(Terri removes her hood. She's a Caucasian woman.)

TERRI: I think you're very beautiful, too.

(Mark starts to remove the rest of his costume.)

At a moment like this, I can't help but wonder, was it all so terribly necessary? Did we have to wander so far afield to reach a point which comes, when it does at last, so naturally?

MARK: I was afraid. I was an Asian man.

TERRI: And I was a woman, of any description.

MARK: Why are we talking as if those facts were behind us?

TERRI: Well, we have determined to move beyond the world of fantasy ... haven't we?

(Mark's costume is off. He stands in simple boxer shorts. Mark and Terri cross the stage toward one another.)

MARK: But tell the truth—would you have dated me? If I'd come to you first like this?

TERRI: Who knows? Anything's possible. This is the 1990s.

(Mark touches Terri's hair. They gaze at each other's faces as lights fade to black.)

END OF PLAY

TRYING
TO FIND
CHINATOWN
(1996)

Production History

Trying to Find Chinatown received its premiere at the
Actors Theatre of Louisville (Jon Jory, Producing
Director), as part of the 20th Annual Humana Festival of
New American Plays, in Louisville, Kentucky, on March
29, 1996. It was directed by Paul McCrane; the set design
was by Paul Owen; the costume design was by Kevin R.
McLeod; the lighting design was by Brian Scott; the sound
design was by Martin Desjardins; the original violin music
was composed by Derek Reeves; the dramaturg was
Michael Bigelow Dixon; and the stage manager was Julie
A. Richardson. The cast was as follows:

BENJAMIN   Richard Thompson
RONNIE   Zar Acayan

Characters

BENJAMIN, Caucasian male, early twenties.
RONNIE, Asian-Amerian male, mid-twenties.

Time and Place

A street corner on the Lower East Side, New York City. The present.

Note on Music

Obviously, it would be foolish to require that the actor portraying Ronnie perform the specified violin music live. The score of this play can be played on tape over the house speakers, and the actor can feign playing the violin using a bow treated with soap. However, in order to effect a convincing illusion, it is desirable that the actor possess some familiarity with the violin or another stringed instrument.

Darkness. Over the house speakers, sound fades in: Hendrix-like virtuoso rock 'n' roll riffs—heavy feedback, distortion, phase shifting, wah-wah—amplified over a tiny Fender pug-nose.

Lights fade up to reveal that the music's being played over a solid-body electric violin by Ronnie, a Chinese-American male in his mid-twenties; he is dressed in retro-'60s clothing and has a few requisite '90s body mutilations. He's playing on a sidewalk for money, his violin case open before him; change and a few stray bills have been left by previous passersby.

Benjamin enters; he's in his early twenties, blond, blue-eyed, a Midwestern tourist in the big city. He holds a scrap of paper in his hands, scanning street signs for an address. He pauses before Ronnie, listens for a while. With a truly bravura run, Ronnie concludes the number and falls to his knees, gasping. Benjamin applauds.

BENJAMIN: Good. That was really great. *(Pause)* I didn't . . . I mean, a fiddle . . . I mean, I'd heard them at square dances, on country stations and all, but I never . . . wow, this must really be New York City!

(Benjamin applauds, starts to walk on. Still on his knees, Ronnie clears his throat loudly.)

Oh, I . . . you're not just doing this for your health, right?

(Benjamin reaches in his pocket, pulls out a couple of coins. Ronnie clears his throat again.)

Look, I'm not a millionaire, I'm just . . .

(Benjamin pulls out his wallet, removes a dollar bill. Ronnie nods his head and gestures toward the violin case as he takes out a pack of cigarettes, lights one.)

RONNIE: And don't call it a "fiddle," OK?

BENJAMIN: Oh. Well, I didn't mean to—

RONNIE: You sound like a wuss. A hick. A dipshit.

BENJAMIN: It just slipped out. I didn't really—

RONNIE: If this was a fiddle, I'd be sitting here with a cob pipe, stomping my cowboy boots and kicking up hay. Then I'd go home and fuck my cousin.

BENJAMIN: Oh! Well, I don't really think—

RONNIE: Do you see a cob pipe? Am I fucking my cousin?

BENJAMIN: Well, no, not at the moment, but—

RONNIE: All right. Then this is a violin, now you give me your money, and I ignore the insult. Herein endeth the lesson.

(Pause.)

BENJAMIN: Look, a dollar's more than I've ever given to a . . . to someone asking for money.

RONNIE: Yeah, well, this is New York. Welcome to the cost of living.

BENJAMIN: What I mean is, maybe in exchange, you could help me—?

RONNIE: Jesus Christ! Do you see a sign around my neck reading "Big Apple Fucking Tourist Bureau"?

BENJAMIN: I'm just looking for an address, I don't think it's far from here, maybe you could . . . ?

(Benjamin holds out his scrap of paper, Ronnie snatches it away.)

RONNIE: You're lucky I'm such a goddamn softy. *(He looks at the paper)* Oh, fuck you. Just suck my dick, you and the cousin you rode in on.

BENJAMIN: I don't get it! What are you—?

RONNIE: Eat me. You know exactly what I—

BENJAMIN: I'm just asking for a little—

RONNIE: "13 Doyers Street"? Like you don't know where
that is?

BENJAMIN: Of course I don't know! That's why I'm asking—

RONNIE: C'mon, you trailer-park refugee. You don't know
that's Chinatown?

BENJAMIN: Sure I know that's Chinatown.

RONNIE: I know you know that's Chinatown.

BENJAMIN: So? That doesn't mean I know where
Chinatown—

RONNIE: So why is it that you picked *me,* of all the street
musicians in the city—to point you in the direction of
Chinatown? Lemme guess—is it the earring? No, I
don't think so. The Hendrix riffs? Guess again, you
fucking moron.

BENJAMIN: Now, wait a minute. I see what you're—

RONNIE: What are you gonna ask me next? Where you can
find the best dim sum in the city? Whether I can direct
you to a genuine opium den? Or do I happen to know
how you can meet Miss Saigon for a night of nookie-
nookie followed by a good old-fashioned ritual suicide?
Now, get your white ass off my sidewalk. One dollar
doesn't even begin to make up for all this aggravation.
Why don't you go back home and race bullfrogs, or
whatever it is you do for—?

BENJAMIN: Brother, I can absolutely relate to your anger.
Righteous rage, I suppose, would be a more appropri-
ate term. To be marginalized, as we are, by a white
racist patriarchy, to the point where the accomplish-
ments of our people are obliterated from the history
books, this is cultural genocide of the first order, leading to the fact that you must do battle with all of Euro-
America's emasculating and brutal stereotypes of
Asians—the opium den, the sexual objectification of
the Asian female, the exoticized image of a tourist's
Chinatown which ignores the exploitation of workers,
the failure to unionize, the high rate of mental illness

and tuberculosis—against these, each day, you rage,
no, not as a victim, but as a survivor, yes, brother, a glorious warrior survivor!

(Silence.)

RONNIE: Say what?

BENJAMIN: So, I hope you can see that my request is not—

RONNIE: Wait, wait.

BENJAMIN: —motivated by the sorts of racist assumptions—

RONNIE: But, but where . . . how did you learn all that?

BENJAMIN: All what?

RONNIE: All that—you know—oppression stuff—tuberculosis . . .

BENJAMIN: It's statistically irrefutable. TB occurs in the
community at a rate—

RONNIE: Where did *you* learn it?

BENJAMIN: I took Asian-American studies. In college.

RONNIE: Where did you go to college?

BENJAMIN: University of Wisconsin. Madison.

RONNIE: Madison, Wisconsin?

BENJAMIN: That's not where the bridges are, by the way.

RONNIE: Huh? Oh, right . . .

BENJAMIN: You wouldn't believe the number of people
who—

RONNIE: They have Asian-American studies in Madison,
Wisconsin? Since when?

BENJAMIN: Since the last Third World Unity hunger strike.
(Pause) Why do you look so surprised? We're down.

RONNIE: I dunno. It just never occurred to me, the idea of
Asian students in the Midwest going on a hunger strike.

BENJAMIN: Well, a lot of them had midterms that week, so
they fasted in shifts. *(Pause)* The administration never
figured it out. The Asian students put that "They all
look alike" stereotype to good use.

RONNIE: OK, so they got Asian-American studies. That still
doesn't explain—

BENJAMIN: What?

RONNIE: Well . . . what *you* were doing taking it?

BENJAMIN: Just like everyone else. I wanted to explore my roots. And, you know, the history of oppression which is my legacy. After a lifetime of assimilation, I wanted to find out who I really am.

(Pause.)

RONNIE: And did you?

BENJAMIN: Sure. I learned to take pride in my ancestors who built the railroads, my Popo who would make me a hot bowl of jok with thousand-day-old eggs when the white kids chased me home yelling, "Gook! Chink! Slant-eyes!"

RONNIE: OK, OK, that's enough!

BENJAMIN: Painful to listen to, isn't it?

RONNIE: I don't know what kind of bullshit ethnic studies program they're running over in Wuss-consin, but did they bother to teach you that in order to find your Asian "roots," it's a good idea to first be Asian?

(Pause.)

BENJAMIN: Are you speaking metaphorically?

RONNIE: No! Literally! Look at your skin!

BENJAMIN: You know, it's very stereotypical to think that all Asian skin tones conform to a single hue.

RONNIE: You're white! Is this some kind of redneck joke or something? Am I the first person in the world to tell you this?

BENJAMIN: Oh! Oh! Oh!

RONNIE: I know real Asians are scarce in the Midwest, but . . . Jesus!

BENJAMIN: No, of course, I . . . I see where your misunderstanding arises.

RONNIE: Yeah. It's called, "You white."

BENJAMIN: It's just that—in my hometown of Tribune, Kansas, and then at school—see, everyone knows me—so this sort of thing never comes up. *(He offers his hand)* Benjamin Wong. I forget that a society wedded to racial constructs constantly forces me to explain my very existence.

RONNIE: Ronnie Chang. Otherwise known as "The Bow Man."

BENJAMIN: You see, I was adopted by Chinese-American parents at birth. So, clearly, I'm an Asian-American—

RONNIE: Even though you're blond and blue-eyed.

BENJAMIN: Well, you can't judge my race by my genetic heritage alone.

RONNIE: If genes don't determine race, what does?

BENJAMIN: Perhaps you'd prefer that I continue in denial, masquerading as a white man?

RONNIE: You can't just wake up and say, "Gee, I *feel* black today."

BENJAMIN: Brother, I'm just trying to find what you've already got.

RONNIE: What do I got?

BENJAMIN: A home. With your people. Picketing with the laundry workers. Taking refuge from the daily slights against your masculinity in the noble image of Gwan Gung.

RONNIE: Gwan who?

BENJAMIN: C'mon—the Chinese god of warriors and— what do you take me for? There're altars to him up all over the community.

RONNIE: I dunno what community you're talking about, but it's sure as hell not mine.

(Pause.)

BENJAMIN: What do you mean?

RONNIE: I mean, if you wanna call Chinatown *your* community, OK, knock yourself out, learn to use chopsticks, big deal. Go ahead, try and find your "roots" in some dim sum parlor with headless ducks hanging in the window. Those places don't tell you a thing about who *I* am.

BENJAMIN: Oh, I get it.

RONNIE: You get what?

BENJAMIN: You're one of those self-hating, *assimilated* Chinese-Americans, aren't you?

RONNIE: Oh, Jesus.

BENJAMIN: You probably call yourself "Oriental," huh? Look, maybe I can help you. I have some books I can—

RONNIE: Hey, I read all those Asian identity books when you were still slathering on industrial-strength sunblock. *(Pause)* Sure, I'm Chinese. But folks like you act like that means something. Like, all of a sudden, you know who I am. You think identity's that simple? That you can wrap it all up in a neat package and say, "I have ethnicity, therefore I am"? All you fucking ethnic fundamentalists. Always settling for easy answers. You say you're looking for identity, but you can't begin to face the real mysteries of the search. So instead, you go skin-deep, and call it a day. *(Pause. He turns away from Benjamin and starts to play his violin—slow and bluesy)*

BENJAMIN: So what are you? "Just a human being"? That's like saying you *have* no identity. If you asked me to describe my dog, I'd say more than, "He's just a dog."

RONNIE: What—you think if I deny the importance of my race, I'm nobody? There're worlds out there, worlds you haven't even begun to understand. Open your eyes. Hear with your ears.

(Ronnie holds his violin at chest level, but does not attempt to play during the following monologue. As he speaks, rock and jazz violin tracks fade in and out over the house speakers, bringing to life the styles of music he describes.)

I concede—it was called a fiddle long ago—but that was even before the birth of jazz. When the hollering in the fields, the rank injustice of human bondage, the struggle of God's children against the plagues of the devil's white man, when all these boiled up into that bittersweet brew, called by later generations, the blues.

That's when fiddlers like Son Sims held their chin rests at their chests, and sawed away like the hillbillies still do today. And with the coming of ragtime appeared the pioneer Stuff Smith, who sang as he stroked the catgut, with his raspy, Louis Armstrong–voice— gruff and sweet like the timber of horsehair riding south below the fingerboard—and who finally sailed for Europe to find ears that would hear. Europe— where Stephane Grappelli initiated a magical French violin, to be passed from generation to generation— first he, to Jean-Luc Ponty, then Ponty to Didier Lockwood. Listening to Grappelli play "A Nightingale Sang in Berkeley Square" is to understand not only the song of birds, but also how they learn to fly, fall in love on the wing, and finally falter one day, to wait for darkness beneath a London street lamp. And Ponty—he showed how the modern violin man can accompany the shadow of his own lead lines, which cascade, one over another, into some nether world beyond the range of human hearing. Joe Venuti. Noel Pointer. Sven Asmussen. Even the Kronos Quartet, with their arrangement of "Purple Haze." Now, tell me, could any legacy be more rich, more crowded with mythology and heroes to inspire pride? What can I say if the banging of a gong or the clinking of a pickax on the Transcontinental Railroad fails to move me even as much as one note, played through a violin MIDI controller by Michael Urbaniak? *(He puts his violin to his chin, begins to play a jazz composition of his own invention)* Does it have to sound like Chinese opera before people like you decide I know who I am?

(Benjamin stands for a long moment, listening to Ronnie play. Then, he drops his dollar into the case, turns and exits right. Ronnie continues to play a long moment. Then Benjamin enters downstage left, illuminated in his own spotlight. He sits on the floor of the stage, his feet

dangling off the lip. As he speaks, Ronnie continues playing his tune, which becomes underscoring for Benjamin's monologue. As the music continues, does it slowly begin to reflect the influence of Chinese music?)

BENJAMIN: When I finally found Doyers Street, I scanned the buildings for Number 13. Walking down an alley where the scent of freshly steamed char siu bao lingered in the air, I felt immediately that I had entered a world where all things were finally familiar. *(Pause)* An old woman bumped me with her shopping bag—screaming to her friend in Cantonese, though they walked no more than a few inches apart. Another man—shouting to a vendor in Sze-Yup. A youth, in white undershirt, perhaps a recent newcomer, bargaining with a grocer in Hokkien. I walked through this ocean of dialects, breathing in the richness with deep gulps, exhilarated by the energy this symphony brought to my step. And when I finally saw the number 13, I nearly wept at my good fortune. An old tenement, paint peeling, inside walls no doubt thick with a century of grease and broken dreams—and yet, to me, a temple—the house where my father was born. I suddenly saw it all: Gung Gung, coming home from his sixteen-hour days pressing shirts he could never afford to own, bringing with him candies for my father, each sweet wrapped in the hope of a better life. When my father left the ghetto, he swore he would never return. But he had, this day, in the thoughts and memories of his son, just six months after his death. And as I sat on the stoop, I pulled a hua-moi from my pocket, sucked on it, and felt his spirit returning. To this place where his ghost, and the dutiful hearts of all his descendants, would always call home. *(He listens for a long moment)* And I felt an ache in my heart for all those lost souls, denied this most important of revelations: to know who they truly are.

David Henry Hwang

(Benjamin sucks his salted plum and listens to the sounds around him. Ronnie continues to play. The two remain oblivious of one another. Lights fade slowly to black.)

END OF PLAY

DAVID HENRY HWANG, is a playwright, screen-writer and librettist. His plays *FOB* (1981 OBIE Award), *The Dance and the Railroad* (1982 Drama Desk nomination), *Family Devotions* (1982 Drama Desk nomination), *The Sound of a Voice* and *The House of Sleeping Beauties*, were all produced at The Joseph Papp Public Theater/New York Shakespeare Festival. His other plays include: *M. Butterfly* (Broadway, 1988 Tony, Drama Desk, Outer Critics, John Gassner awards); *Face Value* (Off-Broadway); *Bondage*; *Trying to Find Chinatown* (both produced by Actors Theatre of Louisville's Humana Festival) and *Golden Child*, which was commissioned by South Coast Repertory, premiered at The Joseph Papp Public Theater/New York Shakespeare Festival, and moved to Broadway (1997 OBIE Award, 1998 Tony, Outer Critics nominations). His adaptation of Ibsen's *Peer Gynt*, written with Stephan Müller, premiered in 1998 at Trinity Repertory Company. His libretti include two works for composer Philip Glass: *1000 Airplanes on the Roof* and *The Voyage*; *The Silver River* with music by Bright Sheng; and with Linda Woolverton and Robert Falls, he has co-authored the book for *Aida*, with music by Elton John and Tim Rice. Mr. Hwang has received fellowships from the Rockefeller and Guggenheim foundations, the National Endowment for the Arts, the New York State Council on the Arts and The Pew/TCG National Artists Residency Program.

9 781559 361729